AMERICA the BEAUTIFUL

ARIZONA

By Ann Heinrichs

Consultants

Dr. Gary Emanuel, Associate Superintendent, Arizona Department of Education, Phoenix

Marshall Trimble, Director, Southwest Studies Program, Maricopa Community Colleges; author of *Arizona* and *Arizona: A Cavalcade of History*

Robert L. Hillerich, Ph.D., Bowling Green State University, Bowling Green, Ohio

CHILDRENS PRESS®

CHICAGO

A Fremont cottonwood along the Paria River in the Vermilion Cliffs Wilderness

Project Editor: Joan Downing
Associate Editor: Shari Joffe
Design Director: Margrit Fiddle
Typesetting: Graphic Connections, Inc.
Engraving: Liberty Photoengraving

Library of Congress Cataloging-in-Publication Data

Heinrichs, Ann.
  America the beautiful. Arizona / by Ann Heinrichs.
    p.   cm.
  Includes index.
  Summary: Introduces the geography, history,
government, economy, industry, culture, historic
sites, and famous people of Arizona.
  ISBN 0-516-00449-2
  1. Arizona—Juvenile literature.
[1. Arizona] I. Title. II. Title: Arizona.
F811.3.H45 1991   90-21118
979.1—dc20   CIP
                                    AC

County buildings, Tucson

TABLE OF CONTENTS

Chapter 1
THE DESERT
FLOWER

THE DESERT FLOWER

Arizona's temperature, said author Mark Twain, "remains at a constant 120 degrees in the shade, except when it varies and goes higher."

Twain might be surprised to see Arizona today. Threaded with irrigation canals, the desert is abloom with vegetables, citrus fruit, and cotton. Though hot, the desert air is comfortably dry. Millions of people visit every year to soak up its warmth.

Arizona is much more than desert, though. Pine forests and cool mountain streams grace its central highlands. Ski tracks snake down its snowy peaks. High plateaus and deep gorges, formed over millions of years, make the northern part of the state a geologist's dream. Arizona takes its nickname—Grand Canyon State—from the most spectacular of these gorges. The Grand Canyon is called one of the seven natural wonders of the world.

Miners found their share of natural wonders in Arizona, too. In the 1800s, copper, silver, and gold drew a stampede of prospectors to the territory. Mining towns sprang up, said Mark Twain, wherever there was "a rumor and a hole in the ground." But boomtowns turned to ghost towns as gold and silver declined. Broken dreams left their trail on the map with names of vacated towns. Copper was the mineral that endured, giving birth to Arizona's manufacturing industries.

Today, Arizona is one of the fastest-growing states in the country. With thriving high-technology plants, tourist spots, and retirement towns, Arizona still blossoms with fresh hopes and dreams.

Chapter 2

THE LAND

THE LAND

The sixth-largest state in the country, covering 114,000 square miles (295,260 square kilometers), Arizona is one of the southwestern states. Its shape is roughly rectangular, with its perfectly straight northern and eastern borders drawn along lines of latitude and longitude. Utah borders Arizona to the north and New Mexico to the east. At Arizona's northeastern tip is a point called Four Corners, where Utah, Colorado, New Mexico, and Arizona meet at right angles. In contrast, the mighty Colorado River defines Arizona's jagged western edge, with Nevada and California across the river to the west. The Mexican state of Sonora forms Arizona's southern boundary.

TOPOGRAPHY

Arizona's elevation generally slopes from northeast to southwest. The state is divided into three major land regions: the Colorado Plateau, the mountain zone, and the desert region. Within each region are many contrasting topographic features.

Extending into Utah, Colorado, and New Mexico, the Colorado Plateau covers the northern and northeastern portions of Arizona. High plateaus and flat-topped mesas mark the Colorado Plateau, while canyons cut deep gashes into the earth's rocky crust. Long-extinct volcanoes have left massive craters, such as Sunset Crater, throughout the region, too. Deserts, hardwood forests, and snow-covered slopes are all found on the Colorado Plateau.

Canyon de Chelly, in the Colorado Plateau

Winding across the state's northwestern portion is the Colorado River. Chiseling through layers of rock over millions of years, the waters of the Colorado formed the Grand Canyon, the deepest of Arizona's spectacular gorges. Other canyons in the plateau are Canyon de Chelly (pronounced "canyon d'shay"), Oak Creek Canyon, and Sycamore Canyon.

The northwestern area, hemmed in by the Colorado River, is called the Arizona Strip. Where the Colorado cuts abruptly to the north, the Little Colorado River curves around to the south, forming a great bend around Arizona's northeastern corner. Within this bend are the Kaibito Plateau; the Black Mesa, with its three fingerlike extensions; and the Painted Desert, with its prehistoric forest of petrified wood. A collection of eerie rock formations at the northeastern Arizona-Utah border has been named Monument Valley.

The West Fork of the Little Colorado River in the White Mountains (left) and Coconino National Forest in the Mogollon Rim (right) are in the mountain zone.

The southern part of the Colorado Plateau is called the San Francisco Plateau. This region, dotted with volcanic cones, has a lower elevation than the land to the north. Among the San Francisco Peaks, however, is 12,633-foot (3,851-meter) Humphreys Peak, the highest point in the state. Flagstaff, directly south of Humphreys Peak, is the largest city on the Colorado Plateau.

South of the Colorado Plateau is the mountain zone—also called the Transition Zone—between the high plateaus and the desert. This narrow northwest-to-southeast strip of land is largely mountainous and forested. A steep-walled ridge called the Mogollon Rim (pronounced "muggy-own") runs across the region's northern boundary. The Mazatzal, Santa Maria, Sierra Ancha, and White mountain ranges rise in this region. Rich

The Santa Catalinas (left) and the Chiricahuas (right) are among the low, heavily forested mountain ranges that are scattered through the state's desert region.

deposits of copper, silver, and gold have been found in these hills. Prescott, in the Bradshaw Mountains, is the region's largest city.

Dropping to a lower elevation, Arizona's desert region, or Basin and Range Region, covers roughly the southwestern half of the state. It extends along the state's western border and widens into the southwest and across the south. The great Sonoran Desert covers the large central portion of this region. The Sonoran Desert is neither all flat nor all dry. Scattered through the desert plains are a number of low, heavily forested mountain ranges. These include the Harcuvar, Castle Dome, Gila, Gila Bend, Sand Tank, Ajo, Baboquivari, Santa Catalina, Santa Rita, Pinaleno, Galiuro, and Chiricahua mountains.

The Gila River and its major tributary, the Salt River, flow through the Sonoran Desert. Aided by irrigation, the fertile Gila

The Little Colorado River is one of the major tributaries of the Colorado River.

and Salt river valleys are among Arizona's most productive agricultural lands. Thus, they were the first areas in the state to draw settlers. Today, Arizona's largest cities—Phoenix, Tucson, Mesa, Tempe, Glendale, and Scottsdale—are located in the desert region and form what is called the Golden Corridor.

RIVERS AND LAKES

The great Colorado River is Arizona's longest and most important river. Including its many large tributaries, the Colorado River system drains more than 90 percent of the state's land area. Flowing from Utah, the Colorado enters Arizona at the center of its northern border, flows west through the Grand Canyon for 277 miles (446 kilometers), and then turns south to form most of Arizona's western border, eventually emptying into the Gulf of California. In all, the Colorado spends 688 miles (1,107 kilometers)

Havasu Falls is one of several waterfalls formed by Havasu Creek.

of its total course in Arizona. Its major tributaries are the Gila, the Little Colorado, and the Bill Williams rivers.

The Gila River, Arizona's second-longest river, flows across the state from east to west and joins the Colorado near Yuma. The Gila has a number of tributaries of its own, including the Salt, Santa Cruz, and San Pedro rivers. The Verde River, rising from springs in Chino Valley, is a tributary of the Salt River.

The Little Colorado River flows through northeastern Arizona, entering the Colorado at the east end of the Grand Canyon. Its major tributaries are the Zuni River, the Rio Puerco, and Lithodendron Creek.

Most of Arizona's smaller rivers are dry during the warmer seasons of the year. Other rivers may appear dry on the surface, while water continues to flow underground. With so many mountains and steep canyons and cliffs, Arizona is adorned by a number of waterfalls. As Havasu Creek in Grand Canyon

National Park drops in elevation, it forms Beaver, Bridal Veil, Havasu, Mooney, and Navajo falls.

Arizona has a few natural lakes, most of them small lakes in the mountainous regions. The majority of the state's lakes are artificial lakes and reservoirs created by damming rivers. Glen Canyon Dam, on the Colorado River, forms Lake Powell, most of which is in Utah. Along Arizona's western border, Lake Mead backs Hoover Dam, Lake Mohave backs Davis Dam, and Havasu Lake backs Parker Dam. Coolidge Dam, on the Gila River, creates San Carlos Lake. Lakes formed by dams on the Salt River include Saguaro, Canyon, Apache, and Theodore Roosevelt.

CLIMATE

Arizona's generally clear, dry climate makes it a comfortable place to live. Throughout much of the state, the climate is typical of all desert regions, with a great contrast between day and night temperatures. At the same time, mountain and desert temperatures vary widely. For example, winter temperatures frequently dip below 0 degrees Fahrenheit (minus 18 degrees Celsius) in the mountains, whereas desert temperatures may not drop below freezing for several years. Statewide, the average temperature in July is 80 degrees Fahrenheit (27 degrees Celsius). January temperatures average 41 degrees Fahrenheit (5 degrees Celsius). The highest temperature ever recorded in Arizona was 127 degrees Fahrenheit (53 degrees Celsius), on July 7, 1905, at Parker. The state's lowest temperature was measured at minus 40 degrees Fahrenheit (minus 40 degrees Celsius) on January 7, 1971, at Hawley Lake.

Overall, Arizona's precipitation is light. (Precipitation includes rain, melted snow, and any other form of moisture.) The state's

Aspens and ponderosa pines are among the trees native to Arizona.

average yearly precipitation is 13 inches (33 centimeters). However, as with temperature, there is wide variation in different parts of the state. Yuma receives an average of only 3 inches (8 centimeters) a year, while McNary in the White Mountains gets as much as 30 inches (76 centimeters). The Golden Corridor cities receive somewhat less than the state's average, with 7 inches (18 centimeters) a year in Phoenix and 11 inches (28 centimeters) a year in Tucson.

PLANTS AND ANIMALS

More than one-fourth of Arizona's land area is covered by forests of aspen, birch, fir, spruce, oak, and pine trees. The biggest stands of ponderosa pine trees in the United States grow in

Aspens (left) grow in Arizona's mountain forests, and a wide variety of cactus plants (right) thrive in the state's southern desert area.

Arizona's mountain forests. The desert area of southern Arizona supports a completely different kind of plant life. There, the tallest plant is the saguaro cactus. Growing as high as 50 feet (15 meters), the saguaro is the largest variety of cactus in the United States. Prickly pear, barrel, cholla, and organ-pipe cactus also grow there, along with yucca, ocotillo, mesquite, and manzanita. The largest of the yucca species is the eerie-looking Joshua tree. More than four hundred edible plants can be found in the Sonoran Desert. Wildflowers such as golden columbines, paint brushes, poppies, and phlox add color to Arizona's landscape.

Black bears, elks, mountain lions, bobcats, lynxes, and ocelots roam through the northern forests. The state has large herds of mule deer and white-tailed deer, as well as many smaller animals

Among the insects, animals, and wildflowers that flourish in Arizona's desert climate are scorpions (top left), chuckwallas (left), Mexican poppies, and owl's clover (above).

such as beavers, foxes, raccoons, squirrels, and a kind of wild pig called the javelina.

The desert is home for many harmless snakes and lizards, but poisonous Gila monsters, rattlesnakes, and coral snakes live there, too. Tarantulas and scorpions also live in the Arizona desert. Harmless desert animals include chuckwallas, which are edible lizards, and collared lizards, which run on their hind legs when they are alarmed. Rattlesnakes live in all parts of the state.

There are more than four hundred kinds of birds in Arizona, including wild turkeys, Gambel's quails, cactus wrens, roadrunners, vultures, and eagles. The streams are full of trout, bass, bluegills, and other freshwater fish.

Chapter 3
THE PEOPLE

THE PEOPLE

POPULATION

Arizona ranks sixth among the states in area but only twenty-ninth in population. According to the 1980 census, the state's population was 2,718,425. Arizona, however, is one of the fastest-growing states in the country. Its population grew 53 percent during the 1970s. At the same time, the population of the United States as a whole grew only 11.4 percent. Arizona's population is estimated to have increased almost another 50 percent during the 1980s, to about 4 million.

If Arizonans were spread evenly across the state, there would be a lot of space between them. There are an average of 24 people per square mile (9 people per square kilometer) in Arizona, while the nation as a whole averages 67 people per square mile (26 people per square kilometer).

POPULATION DISTRIBUTION

Until well into the twentieth century, most Arizonans were spread out across the state's wide-open spaces. In the 1940s, however, Arizona's city dwellers began to outnumber those in rural areas. Today, 84 percent of Arizonans live in cities and towns, while the national average is only 74 percent.

More than three-fourths of Arizona's residents live in the Phoenix and Tucson metropolitan areas. Phoenix, the capital, is the largest city, with a 1980 population of 789,704. Its metropolitan area included 1,509,052 people—more than half the population of the entire state. Scottsdale, Mesa, Tempe, Sun City, Glendale, and Chandler are all part of Phoenix's rapidly growing metropolitan area.

Tucson, the second-largest city, had a 1980 population of 330,537; its metropolitan-area population was 531,443. The heavily populated stretch of land from the Phoenix area to Tucson is often called the Golden Corridor.

WHO ARE THE ARIZONANS?

Hispanics, or people of Spanish or Mexican descent, are Arizona's largest ethnic group. Arizona ranks eighth among the states in number of Hispanic residents. While Hispanics comprise more than 16 percent of Arizona's people, they make up only 6 percent of the nation's total population. About 3 percent of Arizona's people are black.

About 6 percent of Arizonans are Indians (Native Americans). Arizona has the third-highest number of Indian residents—about 160,000—among all the states, after California and Oklahoma. Most live on one of Arizona's twenty Indian reservations. Held in trust by the United States government, these reservations cover some 27 percent of Arizona's total land area.

Fifteen major tribal groups are represented in Arizona. Residing in northeastern Arizona, the Navajos are the most numerous of the state's Indian groups. Other reservations are home to the Hopi, Hualapai, Havasupai, Paiute, Apache, Yavapai, Pima, Maricopa, Tohono O'Odham (formerly called Papago), Yaqui, Mohave, Chemehuevi, Cocopah, and Quechan (Yuma) groups.

Because of its pleasant climate, Arizona is a popular state for retired people. A great number of Arizona's new residents in the

Because of the volume of visitors, services at the striking Chapel of the Holy Cross are no longer held regularly. St. John Vianney, a Roman Catholic church in Sedona, oversees the chapel.

1970s were senior citizens eighty-five years of age or older. Between 1970 and 1980, the number of Arizonans in this age group rose 109 percent. This same age group is estimated to have grown another 164 percent in the 1980s.

Younger people are also attracted to Arizona's sunny climate. During the 1970s, the number of thirty- to thirty-five-year-olds in Arizona increased 107 percent, and the twenty-five- to twenty-nine-year-old age group grew 103 percent. In spite of Arizona's popularity with retired people, the median age of Arizonans in 1988 was thirty-one, while the median nationwide was thirty-two.

RELIGION

Arizona counts Roman Catholic church members as its dominant religious group. In fact, Catholics are the major religious group in all but two Arizona counties. The state's second-largest religious group is the Church of Jesus Christ of Latter-day Saints, also known as the Mormon church. Third in number of members is the Southern Baptist Convention. Other churches with large followings in Arizona are the United Methodist, Lutheran, Episcopalian, Assemblies of God, Christian Churches, and Churches of Christ.

Many Arizona Indians continue to hold to their ancient religious beliefs. Dances and other religious ceremonies accompany important life events such as births, deaths, planting, and harvest, and are part of the fabric of daily life.

POLITICS

Arizona came into the Union in 1912 with most of its voters registered as Democrats. For many years, Arizonans continued to elect mostly Democrats to the governorship, the state legislature, and the United States Senate and House of Representatives. From 1931 through 1951, all of Arizona's governors were Democrats. In seven of the ten presidential elections between 1912 and 1948, Arizonans cast their ballots for the Democratic candidate.

With the growth of cities, especially Phoenix and Tucson, the Republican party began to attract more voters. In 1952, John J. Rhodes was the first Arizona Republican elected to the United States House of Representatives, and Republican Barry Goldwater was elected to the United States Senate. Since the 1952 presidential election, Arizonans have supported the Republican candidate.

While the state's small towns and rural areas remained Democratic, people in the larger cities tended to vote Republican. This made a significant difference in the state's voting patterns because the majority of the state's voters lived in Maricopa County, where Phoenix is located. In 1966, the state reapportioned its legislative districts to represent the population more fairly. This meant that fully half the state legislators would be elected from Maricopa County. In 1967, after reapportionment, the big-city voters were able to elect Republican majorities to both houses of the state legislature. This was the first time Republicans had ever had a majority of the seats.

Chapter 4

THE BEGINNING

THE BEGINNING

Fossils found in northeastern Arizona show that people were living there as early as twelve thousand years ago. Around Naco, near Arizona's Mexican border, archaeologists have unearthed the twelve-thousand-year-old tools and weapons of other early inhabitants. These expert hunters, called Paleo-Indians, tracked bisons, woolly mammoths, mastodons, antelopes, camels, horses, and other prehistoric creatures across the Southwest's grassy plains.

As the climate changed over the centuries, grasslands gradually gave way to deserts, and many of the larger animals became extinct. By about 4000 B.C., nomadic hunters occupied the Grand Canyon region. From split twigs, these people made figures of sheep and antelopes. At the same time, a desert culture had emerged in what is now southern Arizona. The desert people lived in roving bands, hunting smaller game and gathering seeds, berries, and nuts.

After corn (maize) was introduced from Mexico around 2000 B.C., early Arizonans spent part of the year farming. One such group was the Cochise People, so named because their remains were found in southeastern Arizona's Cochise County. In the northern canyons, meanwhile, people called the Basketmakers made their homes in caves and underground dwellings called pit houses.

Petroglyphs in Paria Canyon (left) and pottery shards from the Keet Seel cliff dwelling (right) are remnants of Arizona's ancient Anasazi people.

ANASAZI, HOHOKAM, AND MOGOLLON CULTURES

In the second and third centuries B.C., Arizona's three great prehistoric cultures began to appear: the Anasazi on the northern plateau, the Hohokam in the south-central desert, and the Mogollon in the east-central mountains.

The Anasazis of the northern plateau, descendants of the Basketmakers, first dwelled in caves and later in pit houses sunk into the ground. Eventually, they built multilevel adobe pueblos, much like apartment complexes, with ladders leading from one level to another. The pueblos were often built around a central plaza, and religious ceremonies were held in underground chambers called kivas. The Anasazis were the ancestors of peoples known today as the Pueblo Indians.

The Hopi Indians who live on Arizona's high mesas (above) are believed to be descendants of the Anasazis.

The Anasazis raised corn, beans, cotton, and squash. They decorated their pottery with figures of animals or spiritual creatures. For unknown reasons, the Anasazis moved to the high mesa tops and cliffs around A.D. 1050. In the late 1200s, their culture began to decline, and by about 1450, the Anasazis were gone. By studying tree rings, scientists have learned that a great drought swept through Arizona from 1276 to 1299. Crop failures may have wiped out the Anasazis or forced them to wander away.

Arizona's Hopi Indians are believed to be descendants of the Anasazis. The Hopi village of Oraibi, built on Second Mesa about the year 1100, is the oldest settlement in the United States that has been lived in continuously.

These girls dressed for a ceremony (left) and this woman outside her home (right) are among the Hopis who live on Arizona's Hopi Indian Reservation mesas.

The Hohokams, who flourished in the Salt and Gila river valleys, may have come north from Mexico. Their temples and sunken handball courts resemble those of Mexico's Toltec and Maya peoples. To irrigate the desert soil, the Hohokams dug a complex network of canals from the rivers to their fields. From the Salt River alone, they dug more than 250 miles (402 kilometers) of canals. The Hohokam community thrived on rich harvests of corn, beans, squash, tobacco, and cotton. From desert plants they made food, medicines, and construction materials. Hohokam merchants traded with other Indian groups for needed goods. Skilled craftspeople, the Hohokams wove cotton cloth, made clay pottery, and sculpted stone. Long before the Europeans, they devised a method for etching designs into stone and shells. The Hohokams also built the Casa Grande ("large house"), near Coolidge. This four-story tower, built around A.D. 1350, is the oldest masonry construction project in the world.

The Hohokams flourished until around A.D. 1450, when they, too, disappeared. The reasons may have been drought, disease, hostile neighbors, or salt deposits in their irrigation water. Arizona's Pima Indians are believed to be their descendants. The name Hohokam is a Pima word meaning "vanished ones."

In the mountains and forests of east-central Arizona, the Mogollons hunted game, gathered nuts and berries, and grew corn. They traded with the Hohokams for cotton and were the first Arizonans to make pottery. Their homes were pit houses and, later, masonry structures.

OTHER EARLY ARIZONANS

Other prehistoric Arizonans included the Salado, the Patayan, and the Sinagua people. Relatives of the Anasazis, the Salados occupied cliff dwellings along the Salt River. From the Hohokams, they learned how to build irrigation canals and became successful farmers. Ruins of their homes can be seen today in Tonto National Monument near Roosevelt Lake. The Patayan people lived in the Colorado River Valley of western Arizona and in the Prescott area. They may have been the ancestors of Yuma peoples who live in western Arizona today.

The Sinaguas farmed in the Flagstaff and Verde Valley areas. Their homes, like those of the Anasazis, were cliff dwellings and pueblos. A Sinagua ruin in the Verde Valley, now called Montezuma Castle, is five stories high. Nearby, at Tuzigoot National Monument, is a one-hundred-room Sinagua pueblo.

Montezuma Castle (left) is a Sinagua ruin in the Verde Valley. Both Sinaguas and Anasazis settled in the Wupatki Basin (right) about A.D. 1110.

North of Flagstaff, the Wupatki ruins include hundreds of multistory Sinagua homes.

When nearby Sunset Crater began erupting around A.D. 1064, rich volcanic ash fell to the ground and enriched the soil. Other Indian groups began migrating into Sinagua land to farm. Perhaps feeling crowded, the Sinaguas then moved to the ledges and rim of Walnut Canyon, east of Flagstaff. By about A.D. 1500, the Sinaguas, too, had disappeared.

Around A.D. 1100, a new group of people began migrating into Arizona from northwestern North America. Relatives of Alaska's Athabascan Indians, these nomadic bands hunted game, gathered nuts and berries, and raided other Indian settlements for food. Those who settled on the Colorado Plateau came to be called Navajos, and groups settling farther south were called Apaches.

About A.D. 1100, Apaches (left) and Navajos (right) began migrating into Arizona from northwestern North America.

ARRIVAL OF SPANISH EXPLORERS

No one is absolutely certain who was the first European to enter what is now Arizona. In 1528, an expedition led by Spanish explorer Panfilo de Narváez landed in Florida, hoping to conquer the North American interior. All members of the expedition lost their lives, except for four people: Álvar Núñez Cabeza de Vaca, two men named Castillo and Dorantes, and a North African slave called Estevan. For eight years, the four trekked westward. According to Cabeza de Vaca's journals, they reached Arizona's San Pedro River in 1536 and then headed south to New Spain (now Mexico). Many historians, however, do not believe that Cabeza de Vaca ever set foot in Arizona.

The first European known definitely to have entered what is now Arizona was Franciscan missionary Marcos de Niza, known as Fray Marcos. In 1539, Antonio de Mendoza, the viceroy of New Spain, directed de Niza to explore the lands to the north in search of the legendary Seven Cities of Cibola. According to rumors, the very streets of these Zuni villages were studded with precious jewels and gold.

Scouting the route through the San Pedro River Valley for de Niza was Estevan, now in service to the viceroy. He was to send messages back to de Niza in the form of crosses. The closer he came to the cities of gold, the larger each cross was to be.

Estevan, being something of a magician, commanded wonder and awe along the way. Picking up ornaments as he went along, he trekked onward, dazzlingly attired in feathers and bells. When Estevan reached the Zunis' settlement of Hawikuh, now in New Mexico, he sent back to de Niza a cross as big as a man. After a brief welcome, however, the Zunis killed Estevan.

De Niza, following at a safe distance, claimed the area for Mendoza and made a hasty retreat back to New Spain. Could de Niza tell that Hawikuh was built only of mud and stone? Or did he convince himself that he had seen a city of gold? In any case, the fabulous tales he brought back to New Spain led to a massive armed expedition the following year.

THE CORONADO EXPEDITION

In 1540, Spanish explorer Francisco Vásquez de Coronado led a small army north from New Spain, bringing de Niza along as a guide. Under a sweltering sun, the armor-clad men marched through Arizona, reaching Hawikuh in July. Finding no cities of gold, Coronado sent Pedro de Tovar to search the Hopi villages of northeastern Arizona. Next, he sent García López de Cárdenas to the Hopi region. No gold was to be found, but the Hopis led

Cárdenas to a *gran barranca*—the Grand Canyon. Cárdenas was the first European to gaze upon the magnificent chasm.

After tormenting the Indians for two years, Coronado gave up his quest for the cities of gold and returned to New Spain. Many years passed before Spaniards again ventured into Arizona. On an expedition in 1582, Antonio de Espejo discovered silver near present-day Prescott. Juan de Oñate began an expedition in 1598, claiming much of the Southwest for Spain and bringing back valuable minerals.

SPANISH MISSIONARIES

The next wave of Spaniards to move into Arizona were not fortune hunters but missionaries. In 1629, Spanish Franciscan missionaries, called friars, arrived in the Hopi villages. They planned to convert the Hopis to Christianity, at the same time gaining subjects for Spain. By 1670, there were several Franciscan missions among the Hopi pueblos.

In 1680, Indians in present-day New Mexico rose up against the Spaniards in what is called the Pueblo Revolt. They burned missions and other Spanish settlements and killed missionaries. Arizona's Hopis joined the rebellion, too, destroying the Franciscan missions in Hopi land. The Spanish reconquered New Mexico a dozen years later, but efforts to build missions in distant Hopi land were unsuccessful. To this day, there are no Catholic missions on the Hopi mesas.

THE PADRE ON HORSEBACK

After the Pueblo Revolt, Spanish missionary efforts focused on southern Arizona. In 1687, a Jesuit missionary priest named

San Jose de Tumacacori (above) was one of the more than twenty missions established by Eusebio Francisco Kino, the Padre on Horseback (left).

Eusebio Francisco Kino began his ministry to the Pima and Papago Indians of Pimeria Alta. This region extends from northern Mexico into southern Arizona. Unlike some of the earlier visitors, Kino was humble and kind. Called the Padre on Horseback, he explored much of Arizona and California and established at least twenty-four missions. The most famous of these were San Jose de Tumacacori, built in 1696 north of Nogales, and San Xavier del Bac Mission, south of Tucson.

An expert agriculturist, Kino taught the Indians new ways of farming. He showed them how to raise cattle and sheep, thus establishing Arizona's livestock industry. By the time Kino died in 1711, Spanish explorations in Arizona had quieted down.

INDIAN REVOLTS

Sadly, Padre Kino's kindness died with him. Spanish soldiers continued to treat the Indians harshly, and miners and farmers

Kit Carson (above) was a scout
for Colonel Stephen Watts Kearny
(right) during the Mexican War.

took Indian lands. In 1751, the Pima and Papago Indians of
Pimeria Alta revolted. To keep the peace, the Spaniards
established a presidio, or military post, at Tubac near Tumacacori
Mission. This was the first white settlement in Arizona.
Nevertheless, Apaches destroyed both the Tumacacori and San
Xavier missions.

Soon another kindly soul arrived to minister to the Indians.
Francisco Tomás Garcés, a Franciscan friar, began his missionary
work in Arizona in 1768. Garcés traveled far and wide in his
ministry. He explored the Grand Canyon, visited the mesa-top
Hopi villages, and found important new routes to California.

As more Spaniards came and settled on Indian land, there were
more Indian attacks. In 1775, the year before the American
colonists declared their independence from Great Britain, the
Spaniards built a thick-walled presidio at the present site of
Tucson. The Spanish hold on Arizona began to loosen, though. In
1781, reacting to abuses, Yuma Indians massacred white settlers,
including Garcés, in two settlements at the juncture of the Gila
and Colorado rivers. The settlements were not rebuilt. By the

second decade of the 1800s, the troops of New Spain were busy with another pursuit: fighting Spain for independence.

THE MEXICAN PERIOD

In 1821, after three centuries of Spanish rule, Mexico won its independence. Arizona became part of the new country of Mexico, and the Spanish missionaries were driven out.

With no more Spanish troops to fear, American mountain men, traders, and trappers started moving into Arizona. Many of these Anglos, as they were called, became local or national legends. Among the first Anglos to arrive was a sixteen-year-old runaway named Kit Carson. Others were Sylvester Pattie and his son, James Ohio Pattie. There was Pauline Weaver, an intrepid scout whose mother was an Indian. Another, a gangling preacher named Bill Williams, became a trapper after his Osage wife died.

In 1846, the United States and Mexico went to war. One of the heroes of the war was Colonel Stephen Watts Kearny. Guided by Kit Carson, Kearny led his Army of the West from New Mexico through Arizona to California. Assigned to cut a wagon route through the territory, Arizona's Mormon Batallion, led by Lieutenant Colonel Philip Cooke, used Pauline Weaver as a guide.

After Mexico lost the war in 1848, the two nations signed the Treaty of Guadalupe Hidalgo. The United States gained New Mexico, a vast territory extending from Texas to California on the Pacific Ocean. Reaching as far south as the Gila River, the new lands included most of present-day Arizona. Americans opposed to slavery were afraid that this new territory would become slave territory. Nevertheless, the Senate approved the treaty, and the great westward movement of settlers into the New Mexico Territory began.

Chapter 5

TERRITORIAL DAYS

TERRITORIAL DAYS

Spurred by gold discoveries in California in 1848, many newcomers poured into Arizona hoping to find gold and other precious minerals. Besides the prospectors and miners, there were farmers, business people, and railroad workers. Army troops arrived to build forts to protect the whites from Indian attacks. These new settlers began petitioning Congress to create a separate Arizona territory, but they met with no success.

THE GADSDEN PURCHASE

While the gold seekers were heading West, railroads were heading that way, too. Railroad owners envisioned rail lines stretching from the Atlantic Ocean to the Pacific. During the 1850s, the United States Army Corps of Topographical Engineers, guided by mountain men, began to map out Arizona for future highway and railroad routes. Private and government surveyors swarmed over western mountains and plains. In Arizona, it appeared that the best rail route would run south of the Gila River. Already there was a well-trod wagon road there called the Gila Trail, built by the Mormon Battalion during the Mexican War. Mountains and Indians discouraged travel farther north.

Under pressure from railroad interests, President Franklin Pierce sent diplomat James Gadsden to Mexico in 1853 to negotiate a purchase. Persuaded by Gadsden's offer, Mexico agreed to sell the land south of the Gila River, up to Arizona's and New Mexico's present Mexican border. In 1854, Congress ratified the Gadsden Purchase, paying Mexico $10 million, and work on the railroads began.

Before the railroads were opened, stagecoach lines crossed the territory. In 1857, the San Antonio and San Diego Stage Coach Company's "Jackass Mail" route began running through Arizona. Six mules pulled each coach, and the line ran for about a year. The Butterfield Overland Mail began mail and passenger service from Tipton, Missouri, to San Francisco, California, in 1858. Although owner John Butterfield swore that "nothing on God's earth can stop the U.S. Mail," Chief Cochise and his Chiricahua Apaches stopped it at Apache Pass in 1861. Steamboats were chugging up and down the Colorado River with cargo and passengers, too. They entered the Colorado from the Gulf of California, making stops at Yuma, La Paz, Ehrenberg, and Fort Mojave.

CIVIL WAR

When the Civil War broke out in 1861, several southern states seceded, or withdrew from the Union, forming the Confederate States of America. Many Arizona settlers, especially those south of the Gila River, were from southern states and wanted to join the Confederacy. Rebellion-minded Arizonans raised some Confederate fighting men and sent a delegate to the Confederate Congress.

In February 1862, Captain Sherod Hunter and his Confederate troops from Texas boldly marched into Tucson, where the townspeople cheered them on. Hunter scored a few minor victories before large numbers of Union troops caught up with him. In April, at Picacho Pass, Union cavalry from California battled Hunter's forces. Though this is called the westernmost battle of the Civil War, it was little more than a brief skirmish.

Before the railroads were opened, stagecoach lines provided mail and passenger service through Arizona.

ARIZONA TERRITORY

Since the Gadsden Purchase, Arizonans had petitioned Congress several times to make Arizona a territory separate from New Mexico. On February 14, 1862, Confederate president Jefferson Davis declared the Confederate Territory of Arizona. This, and Arizona's growing fame as a source of mineral wealth, roused the United States Congress to action. A bill was passed establishing the Arizona Territory, and President Abraham Lincoln signed the bill into law on February 24, 1863. Charles D. Poston became Arizona's territorial delegate to Congress. Poston had virtually ruled Tubac when he was operating a mine near the town. Until church officials stepped in, Poston was performing marriages, baptisms, and divorces. As a delegate, Poston worked so faithfully for Arizona's causes that he earned the nickname Father of Arizona.

John N. Goodwin was appointed territorial governor and he and his aides set up a temporary capital at Fort Whipple in Chino

Major John Wesley Powell (left) led expeditions in 1869 and 1871 to navigate and map the Colorado River.

Valley. When the fort was moved a few miles to the south, Goodwin went with it, building a governor's mansion that was the beginning of Prescott. Prescott remained the territorial capital until 1867, when the seat of government was moved to Tucson.

For decades, railroad and army surveyors had helped open up Arizona by penetrating the wilderness and mapping it. No one had yet explored the Grand Canyon, though. In 1869, Major John Wesley Powell set out from Wyoming to navigate and map the Colorado River, including its course through the Grand Canyon. With nine men and four rowboats, the one-armed Powell ran rapids and plunged over falls, successfully completing the first navigation of the Colorado River. Powell led a second expedition in 1871, and his beautiful descriptions began to attract sightseers to the canyon.

INDIAN WARS

Keeping law and order in the new territory was a treacherous job. Arizona's Indian wars had broken out on a large scale in

1861, when rancher John Ward's stepson disappeared from his home near Sonoita Creek. Lieutenant George Bascom marched into the stronghold of Chiricahua Apache chief Cochise and accused him of kidnapping the boy. This incident launched a decade of hostilities between the Chiricahua Apaches and the army.

When army troops withdrew to fight the Civil War, Indian raids continued. In 1863, scout Kit Carson, now an army colonel, was ordered to invade Navajo land in northern Arizona and round up all the Indians there. In 1864, these Navajos were marched into New Mexico, where they were confined at Bosque Redondo.

In 1868, in the last treaty between the United States and an Indian tribe, the Navajos' homeland was finally made a reservation, and survivors were allowed to return.

One by one, other Arizona Indian groups were subdued. Arizona's Hualapais surrendered in 1869. In 1872, Cochise's surviving Chiricahua Apaches were given their homeland as a reservation. That same year, Congress declared that Indian tribes would no longer be considered nations and that no further treaties would be drawn up between the United States and the Indian tribes. The Yavapais surrendered to famous Indian fighter General George Crook in 1873. Three years later, they and the Chiricahua Apaches were moved to the San Carlos Apache Reservation.

Geronimo and his band of Chiricahua Apaches, however, continued to terrorize Arizona's sparse and scattered white settlers. His last Apache raiding party surrendered to General Nelson A. Miles on September 4, 1886. Most of the Chiricahua Apaches were sent to prison camps in Florida and later moved to Alabama and Oklahoma. Geronimo survived at Fort Sill, Oklahoma, until 1909, when he died at the age of eighty. By the

Geronimo (mounted, left) and his group of Chiricahua Apaches surrendered to General Nelson A. Miles on September 4, 1886.

time Geronimo was captured, all of Arizona's Indians had been moved to reservations.

Even during the Indian Wars, settlers were busy developing resources that would be the mainstays of Arizona's economy. These were the "three Cs"—copper, cotton, and cattle.

THE MINING BOOM

Gold and silver discoveries brought thousands of miners into the Arizona Territory. Mining boomtowns popped up almost overnight. Arizona's first big gold strike came in 1858, when prospectors found gold at Gila City. In the next few years, gold was discovered at La Paz, Rich Hill, the Bradshaw Mountains, and Vulture, near Wickenburg. Scout Pauline Weaver made one of Arizona's richest gold strikes in what are now called the Weaver Mountains.

By the 1870s, silver had replaced gold in importance. The rich Silver King Mine opened near Superior in 1875. In 1877, Ed

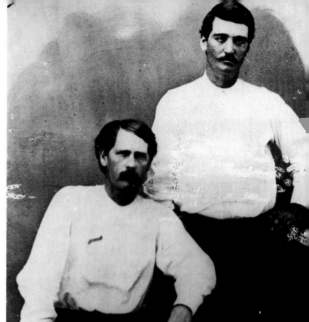

Federal marshal Wyatt Earp (seated) and former marshal Bat Masterson (standing) helped keep the peace in the rowdy mining town of Tombstone (left) in the 1880s.

Schieffelin struck silver in southern Arizona and opened his fabulous Lucky Cuss Mine. Warned that all he'd find there would be his tombstone, Ed named the town that grew there Tombstone. In no time, thousands of fortune hunters flocked in, and saloons and gambling houses opened to entertain them. Famous gunfighters such as Wyatt and Virgil Earp, Doc Holliday, and the Clanton boys helped earn Tombstone its raucous reputation.

Copper soon took over as Arizona's most important mineral find. The rich copper mines of the 1870s and 1880s marked the beginning of Arizona's copper-mining industry. Copper boomtowns included Bisbee, Globe, Miami, Superior, Ajo, Jerome, and Ray. As the mining industries prospered, so did the farmers and ranchers who provided food for all the new mining camps.

FARMING AND RANCHING

In 1867, while passing through the Salt River Valley, prospector Jack Swilling ran across the prehistoric Hohokam irrigation

Laying track for the Prescott and Eastern Railroad in Arizona Territory, about 1898

canals. Gathering together some investors, he had the canals
rebuilt and extended to bring irrigation water into the valley. The
town that grew up around Swilling's operations was named
Phoenix, after a mythical bird that died in flames and then rose up
from its ashes. Like the Phoenix, a town had risen up from the
Hohokam ruins. Cotton, grains, vegetables, and citrus fruit soon
thrived in the reborn river valley.

Texas longhorn cattle were brought in to graze on the ranges,
and ranchers hired cowboys to manage the herds. The typical
cowboy was quite a sight. A Stetson hat shielded him from the
sun, and floppy leather chaps protected his legs from thorny
bushes. In spring roundups, cowboys lassoed new calves and
branded them with the rancher's mark. In months-long cattle
drives, they herded thousands of cattle to markets and railroad
centers. In 1888, Prescott held the nation's first rodeo, where
cowboys could match their skills for prizes. Sheepherders grazed
their sheep on the ranges, too, and cattle ranchers and sheep
owners often fought over grazing lands and water rights.

When the railroads finally arrived in the territory, they gave
Arizona's economy an added boost. The great steam engines of the

Southern Pacific Railroad first chugged into Yuma from California in 1877. Track reached Tucson in 1880, and a spur route to Phoenix opened in 1887. The long-awaited transcontinental rail route crossed northern Arizona in 1883. "Iron horses" changed the pace of life in the Arizona Territory. Now farmers, miners, and ranchers had a faster way to get their goods to market. Railroads made it easier for businesspeople and settlers to get to Arizona, too. Railroad towns blossomed as merchants set up shop to serve the growing population.

THE DRIVE FOR STATEHOOD

In 1877, Arizona's territorial capital was moved from Tucson back to Prescott. It made its final move, from Prescott to Phoenix, in 1889. In the following decade, the territory's economy surged. Arizonans then began to clamor for statehood, but Congress did nothing at that time.

In 1910, Congress passed the Arizona Enabling Act, allowing Arizona to draw up a constitution and apply for statehood. With George W. P. Hunt presiding, delegates gathered in Phoenix for a constitutional convention. They drafted a constitution and submitted it to Congress for approval.

Congress voted in favor of Arizona's statehood in 1911. President William Howard Taft, however, vetoed the Arizona statehood bill. Himself a judge, Taft objected because the constitution allowed judges to be removed by recall, that is, by popular vote. The constitution went back to the convention's delegates, who grudgingly removed the recall clause and resubmitted the document for approval. Finally, on February 14, 1912, President Taft signed the Arizona statehood bill into law, making Arizona the forty-eighth state in the Union.

Chapter 6
THE BABY STATE GROWS UP

THE BABY STATE GROWS UP

When Arizona joined the Union, it completed the solid block of
forty-eight states that stand between Canada and Mexico today.
For the next forty-seven years, until Alaska was admitted in 1959,
the young state of Arizona was fondly called the Baby State.
Arizona was no baby when it came to politics, though. In the first
state election, the people voted to reinstate the recall clause that
had irritated President Taft.

Arizonans elected George W. P. Hunt, chairman of the
constitutional convention, as their first governor. Hunt had come
a long way since he arrived in the Arizona Territory in 1881
without a job. Throughout his seven terms, he worked to develop
dams, roads, and irrigation canals, and he pushed for laws to help
ranchers and miners. Thanks to his efforts, prices for Arizona's
copper remained high through the 1920s.

WORLD WAR I PERIOD

In 1914, European nations became embroiled in World War I.
The United States entered the war in 1917, partly because of the
infamous Zimmerman Note, a secret communication intercepted
by the British. It outlined a German proposal to return Arizona,
New Mexico, and Texas to Mexico in return for Mexico's help in
the war. Arizonans were flabbergasted to hear of the plot. Many
Arizonans marched into battle before the war ended in 1918.

In the Bisbee Deportation, hundreds of miners suspected of belonging to the IWW were herded into railroad cattle cars and shipped to the New Mexico desert.

Arizona's copper, cattle, and cotton industries flourished during the war. At the same time, though, the state was riddled with labor problems. Stirred up by the International Workers of the World (IWW), factory and mine workers staged labor strikes all over the country. When the unrest spread to Arizona's mines, the reaction was swift and stern. In what was called the Bisbee Deportation, a group of armed men in Warren rounded up about twelve hundred miners suspected of being labor-union troublemakers. Then they herded the miners into railroad cattle cars and shipped them into the New Mexico desert.

WATER WARS

Federal conservation projects from 1902 through the 1930s improved Arizona's water-supply problems. With passage of the Reclamation Act in 1902, construction of Theodore Roosevelt Dam on the Salt River began. The project was completed in 1911,

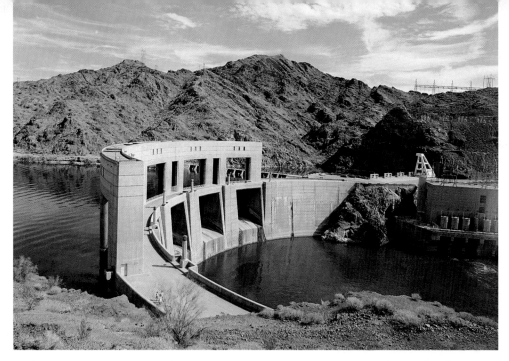

Parker Dam, one of Arizona's many dam projects, supplies water, hydroelectric power, and a water recreation area.

bringing more irrigation water to the desert valley's thirsty soil. Other dams followed, supplying water, hydroelectric power, and water recreation areas. New lakes created by the dams drew visitors to the state, bolstering its tourist trade. Coolidge Dam was erected on the Gila River and Bartlett Dam on the Verde River. On the Colorado River, engineers built Boulder Dam (later renamed Hoover Dam) and Parker Dam.

DEPRESSION AND WORLD WAR II

In the 1930s, when the Great Depression swept the nation, Arizona's population swelled with job seekers from other states. No more jobs were available in Arizona than in the rest of the country, however, and the state's economy took a plunge.

World War II (1939-45) brought the economy back to life. Government contracts set the wheels of Arizona industry in high gear. Arizona's copper was needed for munitions, its cattle

World War II pilots were trained at Davis-Monthan Air Force Base in Tucson.

for beef and leather, and its cotton for uniforms and tents. New factories were built for aircraft and other wartime necessities.

The Army Air Corps found Arizona's clear, sunny skies ideal for training pilots. Ground troops under General George Patton trained in Arizona, too. A prisoner-of-war camp was built outside of Phoenix for captured German submarine crews. There were also retention camps for United States citizens of Japanese ancestry. One such camp was located in Poston, south of Parker.

THE POSTWAR BOOM

In the postwar years, Arizona's population mushroomed. Military personnel returned to raise their families, and cities and suburbs grew. A new invention called air conditioning offset the desert heat. Attracted by the pleasant climate, many retired people settled in the state. Entire cities, such as Sun City northwest of Phoenix, were planned as retirement communities.

Indians' rights expanded in the postwar years. The Arizona

constitution had denied voting rights to the state's Indians. In 1948, this provision was ruled unconstitutional, and Indians finally were granted the right to vote. Indians also enjoyed an economic boom. In the 1960s, several tribes opened businesses, factories, and recreational facilities on their reservations.

In the 1950s, Arizona's population increased 74 percent, and manufacturing began to surpass agriculture as the state's major economic activity. Both industries, however, consumed a lot of water. Factories and farms were relying heavily on Arizona's underground water supply, and rainwater was not falling fast enough for the need. With the skyrocketing population, more homes were using water, too.

MORE WATER PROJECTS

In 1963, the United States Supreme Court ruled in Arizona's favor in a Colorado River water-rights case. This granted Arizona the right to 2,800,000 acre-feet (3.5 billion cubic meters) of water from the Colorado River every year. (One acre-foot is as much water as about five people need in a year.)

In 1968, Congress finally gave its approval to the long-disputed Central Arizona Project. Construction began in 1974, and the system opened in 1985. This project brings water from Lake Havasu on the Colorado River all the way to the Phoenix area. Water service should extend to Tucson by the early 1990s.

As monumental as the Central Arizona Project was, it still did not take care of Arizona's water problems. Most of the project's water was to be used for agriculture, and homes and businesses still used groundwater faster than rain could replace it.

In 1980, the state legislature passed a dramatic water-management law, with stiff penalties for violations. It provides for a gradual decrease in groundwater use, so that the rate of incoming and outgoing water will be balanced by the year 2020.

IN THE POLITICAL SPOTLIGHT

A number of Arizona political figures have drawn national attention. Carl Hayden, born in Tempe, was a United States representative for fifteen years and a senator for forty-two years. During that time, he sponsored the Nineteenth Amendment, for women's voting rights, and pushed through the Central Arizona Project. With fifty-seven years in Congress, Hayden set the record for length of service.

In 1964, the Republican party chose Arizona senator Barry Goldwater as its presidential candidate. In the election, he carried Arizona and five southern states, losing the race to Democrat Lyndon B. Johnson.

Many strong women have helped shape Arizona. One of Arizona's most distinguished women is Judge Lorna Lockwood. A native of Tombstone, Lockwood served fourteen years on Arizona's supreme court. In 1965, she was appointed chief justice, becoming the nation's first woman to head a state supreme court.

Arizona's Hispanic population was proud to have a representative in the state's highest office. Elected in 1975, Raul H. Castro became the first Mexican-American governor of Arizona.

An Arizona woman made history in 1981, when President Ronald Reagan appointed Arizona judge Sandra Day O'Connor to the United States Supreme Court. O'Connor was the first woman ever to sit on the nation's highest court. There she joined another Arizonan, William Rehnquist, a Phoenix attorney who was named to the Supreme Court bench in 1971. In 1986, Rehnquist was appointed chief justice of the Supreme Court.

Arizonans Sandra Day O'Connor and William Rehnquist were appointed to the United States Supreme Court.

Governor Evan Mecham thrust Arizona into the national spotlight in 1988 when he was impeached and removed from office. Secretary of State Rose Mofford succeeded him, becoming Arizona's first woman governor.

INDIAN ISSUES

In 1974, Congress settled a land dispute between the Hopis and Navajos of northeastern Arizona. Land that they had jointly occupied since 1962 was partitioned so that each group had clear boundary lines. Many Indian familes, mostly Navajo, had to be relocated. In 1986, the Hopis officially took possession of their portion of the land. Disputes, lawsuits, and relocations continue as more Navajos are forced to move.

Indians in Arizona, and all over the country, welcome Congress's moves toward American Indian federalism. This would make each organized tribe a self-governing unit, removed from United States government control. Meanwhile, Arizona's Indians struggle into the 1990s with ongoing concerns over land management, employment, education, and self-rule.

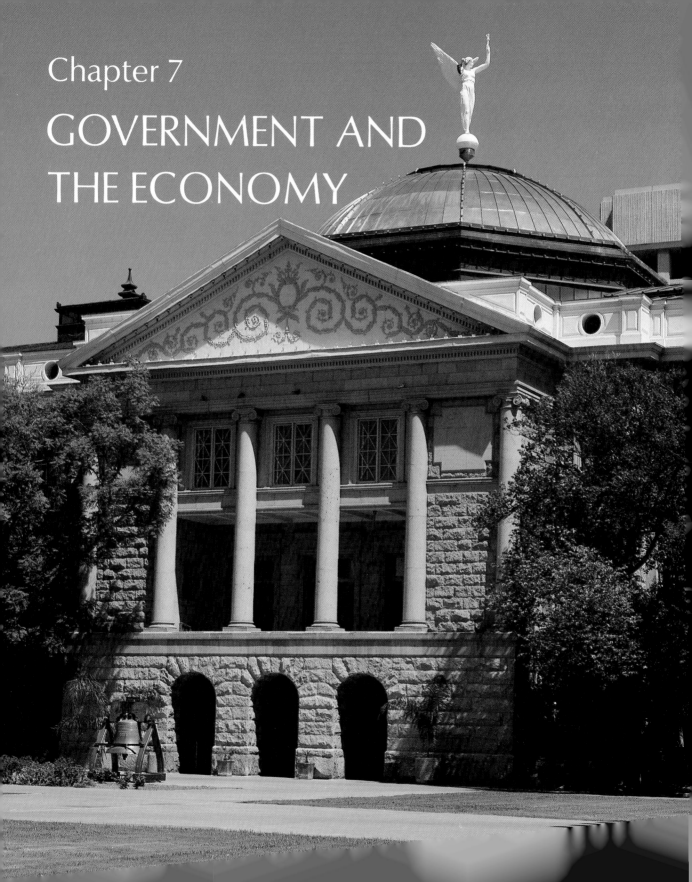

Chapter 7
GOVERNMENT AND THE ECONOMY

GOVERNMENT AND THE ECONOMY

STATE GOVERNMENT

Arizona is still governed by its original constitution. Since its adoption in 1910, the constitution has been amended about ninety times.

Arizona's state government, like the federal government, is divided into legislative, executive, and judicial branches. The legislative branch makes state laws, the executive branch enforces or carries out the laws, and the judicial branch interprets the laws.

There are two houses in Arizona's legislature, a senate and a house of representatives. Every two years, each of the state's thirty legislative districts elects one senator and two representatives to the state legislature. All legislators serve two-year terms.

The governor, head of the executive branch, is elected to a four-year term and can be reelected any number of times. There is no executive office of lieutenant governor. An unexpected vacancy in the governor's office is filled by another elected executive officer. The order of succession is secretary of state, attorney general, state treasurer, and superintendent of public instruction.

Arizona's courts make up its judicial branch. Every county in Arizona has its own superior court, which tries all major cases in the county. Judges in these superior courts serve four-year terms. In Maricopa and Pima counties, where Phoenix and Tucson are located, the governor appoints the judges. In other counties, superior court judges are elected by the people.

Someone who is unhappy with a superior court ruling can appeal to have the case heard again in a higher court, the court of appeals. The court of appeals has twelve judges hearing cases in Phoenix and three in Tucson. Judges are appointed to the court of appeals by the governor for a six-year term. After the first term, people vote whether or not to retain each judge.

From the court of appeals, a case can go to the highest court in the state, the supreme court. The five supreme court justices are appointed by the governor to their first six-year term. The people vote later on retaining supreme court justices. A chief justice is elected by all the justices to a five-year term.

Coconino County, whose county seat is Flagstaff, is the second-largest county in the country. Each of the state's fifteen counties elects its own three-person board of supervisors to two-year terms. The county board of supervisors governs small communities and any unincorporated towns in the county. However, any town of at least fifteen hundred people may vote to incorporate itself. An incorporated town or city can then set up its own government. Arizona has about eighty towns and cities.

EDUCATION

Spanish missionaries opened Arizona's first schools in the late 1600s, teaching mainly religion to the Indians. Arizona's first territorial constitution provided for free public education, and in 1864, the first public school opened in Prescott. Now, as Arizona's high-technology industries grow, state officials hope to prepare Arizona's young people to compete successfully for jobs. Almost two-thirds of the state's revenues are earmarked for education.

Arizona law requires children to attend school from age eight to age sixteen and to complete the tenth grade. About 595,000

The University of Arizona, in Tucson

students are enrolled in Arizona's public schools. Each school
district in the state offers special programs for both gifted students
and students with learning disabilities. About 53,000 disabled
students are enrolled in special education programs.

Arizona has three state universities. The largest is Arizona State
University in Tempe, followed by the University of Arizona in
Tucson and Northern Arizona University in Flagstaff. Arizona
State and the University of Arizona are members of the Pac-10
conference of western universities.

The state-supported Arizona Community College System, one
of the largest in the nation, provides a broad occupational and
community-oriented curriculum. The system operates fifteen
colleges and many other educational centers throughout Arizona.
Arizona has a number of other private colleges and universities,
including the American Graduate School of International

This open-pit copper mine in Hayden contributes to Arizona's standing as the nation's major supplier of copper.

Management in Glendale, Western International University and Grand Canyon University in Phoenix, and Prescott College in Prescott.

MINING AND MINERALS

The quest for precious minerals lured Arizona's first explorers into the region. In Arizona today, mining produces about $1.5 billion a year in metal and nonmetal materials. This accounts for 3 percent of the gross state product. (The gross state product is the total value of goods and services produced in the state in a year.)

Arizona is the nation's major supplier of copper. Its mines produce about $1 billion worth of copper each year—about two-thirds of the national total. The copper comes from both open-pit and underground mines. Some of the major copper-mining locations in the state are San Manuel, Tucson, Morenci, Globe,

Miami, and the Ray pit in Pinal County. Purifying the copper ore yields large amounts of gold, molybdenum, and silver. Other valuable metals include zinc, lead, and uranium.

Because of Arizona's rapid population growth, the mining of sand and gravel, which are used in construction, is a leading mining enterprise. Coal is another of Arizona's valuable mining products, with mines located in Navajo County. Other important nonmetals include lime, pumice, mica, perlite, asbestos, gypsum, petroleum, and gemstones.

MANUFACTURING AND TECHNOLOGY

Sixteen percent of Arizona's gross state product comes from manufacturing. There are more than 3,200 manufacturing plants in the state. Nearly 90 percent of them are located in and around Phoenix and Tucson. These cities attract manufacturers because they can supply a pool of skilled laborers and an inexpensive source of electricity.

High-technology industries find Arizona's dry air an ideal environment for producing high-quality electronic components. Fifteen percent of Arizona's labor force works in manufacturing industries. Almost half of these factory workers are employed in high-technology plants that make aerospace equipment, computers, and electronic equipment.

The production of electrical equipment and machinery is Arizona's leading industry. Every year, products worth about $1.3 billion are made. The state's next most important industries are the production of nonelectrical machinery and transportation equipment. Other important manufactured items include primary metals, printed materials, food and food products, fabricated metals, lumber products, and stone, clay, and glass products.

Grand Canyon National Park draws more than four million tourists a year.

SERVICE AND TOURISM INDUSTRIES

More than 70 percent of Arizona's workers are employed in the state's service industries. These include wholesale and retail trade, community and social services, government, finance, insurance, and real estate. A great number of the state's service employees hold jobs that are related to tourism.

Arizona has more national parklands than any other state, and its delightful weather attracts vacationers from all over the world. Every year, more than twenty million tourists visit Arizona. Grand Canyon National Park alone draws more than four million tourists a year. About half a million of those visitors are from outside the United States. Thus, tourism plays a major role in the state's economy. Arizona's so-called hospitality industries encompass its resorts, inns, dude ranches, hotels, restaurants, nightclubs, and bed-and-breakfast establishments.

The federal government employs large numbers of people at its military bases, such as Williams Air Force Base and Yuma Proving Ground. Government employees also staff the state's twenty Indian reservations.

Harvesting lettuce on the Colorado River Indian Reservation

AGRICULTURE

Arizona has about eight thousand farms, ranging from small truck farms that grow vegetables to huge cattle ranches. Most farming in the state is aided by irrigation. Agriculture accounts for 1 percent of Arizona's gross state product. More than half of this amount comes from crops, even though only about 1.5 percent of the state's land area is used to grow crops. One of the leading cotton-producing states, Arizona ranks first in the production of pima cotton, developed on the Pima Indian Reservation. Cotton is grown between Phoenix and Tucson, in the south-central part of the state. Arizona is the country's second-largest producer of lettuce, cauliflower, and lemons. It ranks third in production of oranges, tangerines, grapefruit, honeydews, and broccoli. Arizona's farmers also grow feed crops, including hay, sorghum grain, barley, and corn.

About 75 percent of the state's total land area is used for grazing herds of cattle and sheep. Much of this rangeland is in the Colorado Plateau, the central highlands, and the Patagonia foothills near the Mexican border. Apaches raise cattle on the San

Cattle at the White River, on the Fort Apache Indian Reservation

Carlos and Fort Apache reservations. Altogether, Arizona's livestock herds number about 1 million head of cattle and 300,000 sheep. More range cattle are shipped from the railroad town of Willcox than from any other place in the world. Livestock and livestock products, in order of importance, are beef cattle, dairy products, poultry and eggs, and sheep and lambs.

TRANSPORTATION

In 1877, the Southern Pacific built the state's first railroad line, into Yuma. A transcontinental railroad crossed northern Arizona in 1883. Then settlers were able to ship their products to other parts of the country, and merchants and business people could bring their goods and equipment in. Now Arizona is crossed by 1,600 miles (2,575 kilometers) of railroad track. Although passenger traffic is not as important as it once was, the railroads are still heavily used for shipping freight. The mining industry especially relies on the railroads to carry loads of copper, sand, gravel, and other products.

In 1919, Tucson became the first city in the United States to have its own city airport. Today, Phoenix's Sky Harbor International Airport is one of the nation's busiest airports. Eighteen major airlines serve Arizona, and about two hundred airports operate throughout the state. Many Arizonans also fly their own private planes.

Over the years, Arizona's scout trails and wagon routes gradually gave way to paved highways. Now, the state has about 77,000 miles (123,916 kilometers) of paved roadways. The old Gila Trail to California became U.S. Route 80, then Interstates 10 and 8. Interstate 17 is the main north-south route through Arizona, from Flagstaff to Phoenix. An east-west road across northern Arizona, opened in the 1850s by adventurer Ned Beale and his fleet of camels, became the fabled Route 66 and eventually Interstate 40. The Grand Canyon is a big natural obstacle to direct highway travel in the northwestern part of the state.

COMMUNICATION

In 1859, Arizona's first newspaper, the *Weekly Arizonian*, began publication in Tubac, south of Tucson. Today the state has about sixty weekly newspapers and a dozen dailies. Those with the largest circulations are Phoenix's *Arizona Republic* and *Gazette* and Tucson's *Arizona Daily Star* and *Citizen*. Of the state's many magazines, *Arizona Highways*, published by the state highway department, is known around the world for its color photography.

Phoenix's KTAR, the first radio station in the state, began broadcasting in 1922. Now there are about ninety radio stations in Arizona. Since the state's first television station, KPHO-TV, started in Phoenix in 1949, the number of television stations has grown to seventeen.

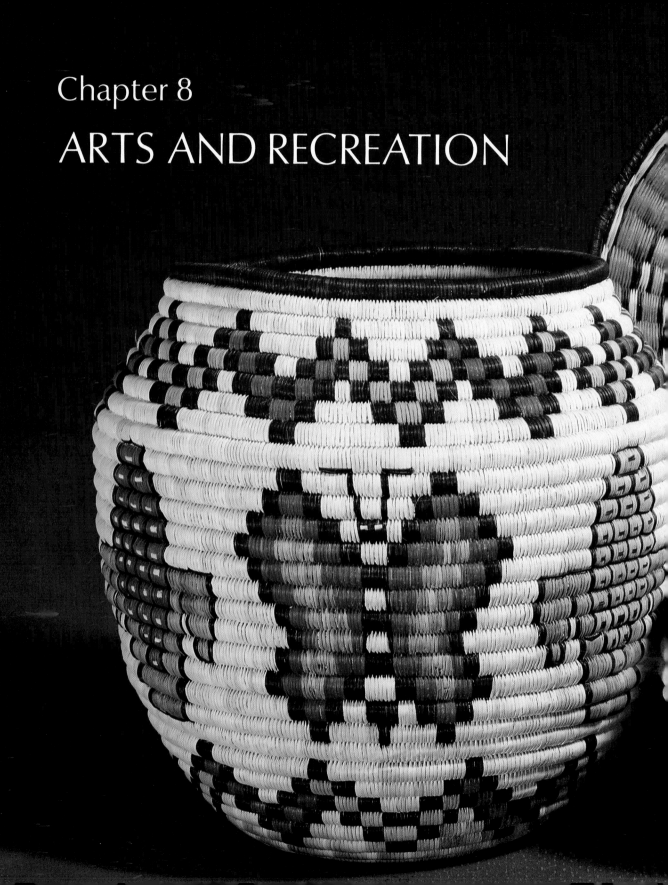

Chapter 8
ARTS AND RECREATION

ARTS AND RECREATION

FINE ARTS

Artists' colonies thrive throughout Arizona. Artists can be seen at work in Sedona, Oak Creek Canyon, Scottsdale, Jerome, Tucson, Lakeside, Bisbee, and Tubac. Scottsdale has one of the highest concentrations of commercial art galleries in the country. Groups of artists in Phoenix, Tucson, and other cities have also banded together to run cooperative galleries.

Arizona's artists follow both realistic and abstract styles. Many artists use Indian or Mexican designs and western themes in their work. Many, too, use the soft or vivid colors of Arizona's landscapes: yellow, ochre, red, purple, blue, and mauve.

Some of the first paintings of Arizona landscapes were rendered by Thomas Moran, who traveled on John Wesley Powell's expedition. Moran's *The Grand Canyon of the Yellowstone* and *The Chasm of the Colorado* hang in the Capitol in Washington, D.C.

Maynard Dixon was known for his drawings, paintings, book illustrations, and murals depicting Arizona scenes. As a young adult in the early 1900s, discouraged to find that only fictionalized views of the West were in demand, Dixon wrote to a friend, "I am being paid to lie about the West." On retiring to his beloved Arizona in 1939, Dixon painted as he wished, capturing the play of light and color on the landscape until his death in 1945.

In the 1880s and 1890s, the famous western artist and sculptor Frederic Remington traveled in Arizona, painting vivid scenes of

Navajo sand painter Art Etcitty creating a work of art at the Hubbell Trading Post in Ganado

his surroundings. Ted De Grazia, an Arizona miner's son, was another popular artist who painted Arizona scenes.

In 1907, sculptor Solon Borglum's monumental bronze statue honoring the famous Rough Riders of the Spanish American War was erected in Prescott's city square. It is considered one of the best equestrian statues in the world. In the early 1980s, citizens of Prescott embarked on a project to commission several more sculptures that commemorate Prescott's rich heritage.

NATIVE ARTS AND CRAFTS

Native American pottery is strikingly different from the potteries of other cultures. Instead of using a potter's wheel to make a pot from a lump of clay, many American Indians coil a "rope" of clay round and round to form a pot. Then they scrape the sides of the pot to smooth the coil's ridges.

In the early decades of the twentieth century, a potter named Nampeyo researched early Hopi pottery and labored to revive ancient techniques and styles. Pottery techniques in Arizona have also been influenced by Maria Martinez, of New Mexico's San Ildefonso Pueblo. Her black-on-black pottery is widely imitated.

According to Navajo legend, the Spider Woman first taught Navajo women the art of weaving. To honor her, Navajo weavers used to leave a little hole in each blanket, like a spiderweb's hole. Eventually, traders insisted that the Navajo weavers forsake the spider hole because it looked like a defect. Today, colorful Navajo rugs and "chief blankets" are prized by collectors throughout the world.

Arizona's Indians use the same basketry techniques that their ancestors used centuries ago. Some baskets are formed by coiling plant fibers, others by weaving them. Flat, round trays and bowl-like vessels are the principal basketry products.

The Hopis and Navajos are expert silversmiths. Their necklaces, bracelets, rings, and buckles are sold throughout the state. The Navajos make concha belts, and their jewelry is often studded with turquoise. Silver overlays and the bear-claw design are hallmarks of Hopi jewelry.

Wood-carved and decorated kachina dolls are representations of the Hopis' spirit gods. The Navajos' sand paintings recall their use of sand designs in religious ceremonies.

ARCHITECTURE

In Arizona, architecture is an ancient art. The earliest Arizonans were master architects, building multiunit masonry dwellings on mesa tops, in caves, and under cliffs. Their thick-walled, flat-topped pueblos inspired Arizona's pueblo style of architecture.

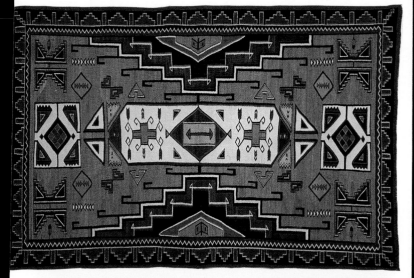

This selection of Arizona's Native American arts and crafts includes (clockwise from top left) a beautifully woven Navajo rug; a Hopi Kachina doll; a silver bracelet and a bola tie that are set with turquoise, lapis lazuli, jet, coral, and ivory made by Navajo Raymond Yazzie; and finely coiled baskets made by San Carlos Apache Gusta Thompson.

Arizona settlers discovered that the thick mud bricks of adobe construction kept their homes cool in the summer and warm in the winter.

Spanish mission churches in Arizona were modeled after those in Mexico. They featured high arches, vaulted and domed ceilings, and two domed bell towers. Many other mission buildings surrounded a central patio or plaza. In Arizona today, there are both churches and secular buildings built in the style of the missions and other Spanish colonial buildings.

Spanish missionaries taught the Indians to build homes of adobe bricks, made of mud and straw and baked in the sun. Later settlers in Arizona adopted adobe construction for their homes. The thick mud bricks kept their homes cool in the summer and warm in the winter. Today, many homes, businesses, and public buildings throughout Arizona are modified adobe structures.

Arizona's modern steel, concrete, and glass structures rise in startling contrast to the older white and sand-colored buildings. These structures are especially stunning against a backdrop of desert and mountains, as in downtown Phoenix.

Taliesin West, in Paradise Valley near Scottsdale, was the western home, studio, and architecture school of master architect

Frank Lloyd Wright. The complex, spread over 600 acres (243 hectares), blends Wright's famous Prairie Style with Arizona's rugged landscape. Wright died in Phoenix in 1959.

Arcosanti, near Cordes Junction, is another architectural wonder. This futuristic, energy-efficient village, and its companion Cosanti in Scottsdale, are the work of visionary architect Paolo Soleri.

LITERATURE

Many of Arizona's early Spanish explorers left written records of their discoveries. Journals or diaries recount the explorations of Marcos de Niza, Francisco Vásquez de Coronado, Antonio de Espejo, Juan de Oñate, and padres Kino and Garcés. Later, mountain man James Ohio Pattie recalled his travels in Arizona in *The Personal Narrative of James O. Pattie.*

More than any other writer, novelist Zane Grey emblazoned an impression of Arizona in the minds of the reading public. Settling in a cabin on the Mogollon Rim in 1908, he fashioned thrilling tales with Arizona settings in western novels such as *The Last of the Plainsmen* and *The Call of the Canyon.*

After working on archaeological digs and studying the Navajos in the 1920s, Oliver La Farge wrote his Pulitzer prizewinning novel *Laughing Boy*, a tribute to the Navajos' loss of their ancient ways. He later published *Enemy Gods*, also with an Indian theme.

Artist and novelist Ross Santee settled in Arizona in 1915, working as a ranch hand for many years. Santee wrote *Lost Pony Tracks, Apache Land,* and several other novels.

Will Levington Comfort was only passing through Arizona when he ran across an old newspaper article about Apache chief Mangas Coloradas, who died during the Apache wars. Comfort became so engrossed with Mangas's life that he immortalized the chief in his 1931 novel *Apache*.

In 1905, when Congress was considering admitting Arizona and New Mexico to the Union as one state, poet Sharlot Hall wrote a passionate poem of protest. Read aloud in the House of Representatives, the poem impressed legislators with a vision of Arizona as a unique and separate land. *Cactus and Pine* and *Poems of a Ranchwoman* are collections of Hall's poems.

Laura Adams Armer received the Newbery Medal in 1932 for *Waterless Mountain*, a children's story about Arizona's Indians.

PERFORMING ARTS

Arizona's major orchestra is the Phoenix Symphony Orchestra. Both Tucson and Flagstaff also support local orchestras, as do a number of other communities in the state. The Arizona Opera Company, the state's only professional opera group, brings a season of opera to both Phoenix and Tucson. Jazz lovers enjoy Scottsdale's Jazz in Arizona concerts, Sedona's Jazz on the Rocks, and the Tucson Jazz Festival.

Professional, semiprofessional, and community theater groups thrive in Arizona, especially in the larger cities. The Arizona Theatre Company, the state's only resident professional drama group, stages shows in both Phoenix and Tucson. Scottsdale's Actors Lab Arizona and the Actors Theatre of Phoenix are smaller professional companies. The Phoenix Little Theatre is the nation's oldest community theater company.

Classical, modern, and ethnic dance troupes perform throughout the state. Phoenix's Ballet Arizona, Tucson's Ballet Arts Foundation, and the Yuma Ballet Theatre and Performing Arts Company specialize in classical dance. Arizona's modern

Mexican children dancing at a fiesta at the Tumacacori Mission

dance companies include the Center Dance Ensemble in Phoenix, Desert Dance Theatre in Tempe, and Orts Theatre of Dance and Tenth Street Danceworks in Tucson. Tucson's Aires Flamencos and Phoenix's Artes Bellas entertain with colorful flamenco performances. Mexican folkloric dance troupes are found throughout Arizona.

FESTIVALS AND CELEBRATIONS

Arizona's western, Mexican, and Native American festivals reflect the state's rich ethnic and historic heritage. Rodeos have been part of the Arizona scene ever since Prescott held the nation's first rodeo. Today, famous rodeo stars ply their craft at the Fiesta de los Vaqueros in Tucson and the Jaycees' Rodeo of Rodeos in Phoenix. Arizonans revel in their frontier heritage during Wyatt Earp Days in Tombstone, the Old Fashioned Mining Camp Celebration in Bisbee, Frontier Days in Prescott, and Gold Rush Days in Wickenburg.

Because of Arizona's large Hispanic population, Mexican national holidays are statewide celebrations. Cinco de Mayo

(May 5) and Dieciseis de Septiembre (September 16) are major Mexican festivals. The annual International Mariachi Festival in Tucson is a musical celebration of the state's Mexican heritage.

On Indian reservations, many traditional ceremonial dances are open to the public. The White Mountain All-Indian Powwow Rodeo and Dances are held on the Apache reservation in June. Flagstaff hosts the Southwest All-Indian Powwow in July. Native American arts of the Four Corners area are featured in the seven-week Festival of Native American Arts in Flagstaff. The Navajo Tribal Fair in Window Rock is held in September.

Easter Sunday morning brings thousands to the Shrine of the Ages on the Grand Canyon's south rim to witness the Easter Sunrise Service. All Souls' Day, November 2, is the occasion for the Day of the Dead Festival in Mesa.

SPORTS

Arizona's sunshine, lakes, and mountains encourage Arizonans and visitors alike to enjoy the great outdoors. Boating, swimming, waterskiing, and fishing are popular activities at the state's large lakes, and thousands of golfers play Arizona's beautiful courses. Although the state isn't thought of as a winter sports haven, skiers enjoy the Fairfield Snowbowl near Flagstaff and Mount Lemmon outside Tucson. Tennis, hiking, and biking are also popular.

Arizona's climate makes it an ideal spot for sporting events. As of 1988, Arizona had its own professional football team—the National Football League Phoenix Cardinals. Formerly based in St. Louis, Missouri, the Cardinals are the nation's oldest football franchise. After summer training in Flagstaff, the team plays its home games in Tempe's Sun Devil Stadium. In 1968, the Phoenix Suns joined the National Basketball Association. The Arizona

Veterans' Memorial Coliseum hosts the Suns' home games.
During hockey season, the same coliseum is filled with hockey
fans cheering the Phoenix Roadrunners.

Spring training season finds eight major-league baseball teams,
informally known as the Cactus League, working out under
Arizona's clear skies. American League ball clubs that train in the
state are the Cleveland Indians, in Tucson; the Milwaukee
Brewers, in Chandler; the Seattle Mariners, in Tempe; the
California Angels, in Mesa; and the Oakland Athletics, in
Phoenix. In the National League, the San Francisco Giants train in
Scottsdale, the Chicago Cubs in Mesa, and the San Diego Padres in
Yuma. Professional golfers are attracted to Arizona's many well-
groomed golf courses. Both the Professional Golf Association and
the Ladies Professional Golf Association regularly include
Arizona courses on their tours. The state also hosts men's and
women's professional tennis tours.

Chapter 9

HIGHLIGHTS OF THE GRAND CANYON STATE

HIGHLIGHTS OF THE GRAND CANYON STATE

Arizona has something for every taste, whether it be beauty, adventure, luxury, or lore. This brief tour of the state highlights Arizona's major points of interest.

INDIAN COUNTRY

The rugged plateaus of northeastern Arizona are home to the Navajo and Hopi Indians. The Navajos' reservation is the largest in the state, completely surrounding the land of the Hopi. Along the northernmost reaches of Navajo land, and extending into Utah, is Monument Valley. Towering above the valley floor is a spectacular array of sandstone spires with red and golden hues. West of Monument Valley is Navajo National Monument. The state's largest collection of prehistoric cliff dwellings, it encompasses the ruins of Betatakin, Keet Seel, and Inscription House.

In the center of Navajo land is the Hopi reservation. High atop First Mesa, Second Mesa, and Third Mesa along Arizona Highway 264 are the Hopi villages. The village of Oraibi, on Third Mesa, is the oldest settlement in the United States that has been lived in continuously. A number of Hopi festivals featuring colorful kachina dancers are open to visitors. The Hopi Cultural Center on Second Mesa sells Hopi pottery, kachina dolls, silver jewelry, and other traditional crafted items.

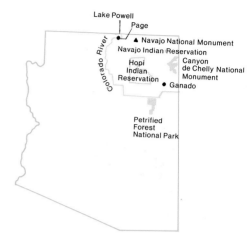

Monument Valley, with its spectacular array of red and gold sandstone spires, extends into Utah from the northernmost reaches of Navajo land.

On the eastern extreme of Navajo land is Canyon de Chelly National Monument. Along the canyon walls are cliff dwellings of Indians who lived there between A.D. 350 and 1300. On the canyon floor, smoke rises from the hogans of Navajo families that live there today.

South of Canyon de Chelly in Ganado is Hubbell Trading Post, a national historic site. Hubbell is the nation's oldest continuously operating Navajo trading post. Besides selling jewelry, rugs, baskets, and other Navajo craftwork, the post offers ordinary grocery-store fare.

Farther south, skirting Interstate 40 east of Holbrook, is Petrified Forest National Park. It contains the largest array of

Spider Rock, at Canyon de Chelly National Monument on the eastern edge of the Navajo Indian Reservation

petrified wood in the world. Unfortunately, souvenir hunters carried away much of the glistening forest before the plundering was outlawed. Now rangers may check cars as visitors leave the park. The oldest dinosaur bones ever discovered were found here, too. Gertie, as the creature is named, roamed the forest 225 million years ago. Across the northern end of the park is the Painted Desert, its hills and rock formations striped in pink, orange, yellow, and gray.

Bordering the northwest corner of the Navajo Reservation is Glen Canyon National Recreation Area, most of which lies in Utah. Flooding the canyon is Lake Powell, formed by Glen Canyon Dam on the Colorado River. Some vacationers at Lake Powell rent houseboats and spend days exploring the waters that wash the canyon's walls. Others enjoy waterskiing, sailing, fishing, and swimming. In the nearby town of Page, visitors to the

Petrified Forest National Park contains the largest array of petrified wood in the world. Polished petrified wood gleams like a precious stone (inset).

John Wesley Powell Memorial Museum can trace his historic trek down the Colorado River.

CANYON COUNTRY

Hundreds of canyons and gorges mark Arizona's northwest corner. The grandest of them all is the Grand Canyon. Branching off from it are countless side canyons, with waterfalls, rapids, and pools.

About six million years ago, the Colorado River began cutting the gorge that is now the Grand Canyon. Now the canyon measures 217 miles (349 kilometers) long, 10 miles (16 kilometers) from rim to rim at its widest, and nearly a mile (1.6 kilometers) at its deepest. Paleo-Indians were the first to gaze upon the canyon, followed by the Spaniards. In 1869, John Wesley Powell, the first

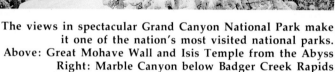

The views in spectacular Grand Canyon National Park make
it one of the nation's most visited national parks.
Above: Great Mohave Wall and Isis Temple from the Abyss
Right: Marble Canyon below Badger Creek Rapids

to chart the area, led a nine-man scientific expedition down the
Colorado River. Today, Grand Canyon National Park is one of the
nation's most visited national parks.

The canyon's north rim is 8,200 feet (2,500 meters) high—1,200
feet (366 meters) higher than the south rim. Travelers who drive
an extra 215 miles (346 kilometers) to the north rim are rewarded
with fabulous views, as well as hiking and camping spots. Hardy
hikers can cross the canyon to the north rim in about three days.
Because of dangerous snows, however, the north rim is closed
from the first snowfall until the middle of May.

Most visitors go to the south rim, since it is easier to reach.
Lining the rim are lodges, restaurants, and viewing points, many
with telescopes. Mather Point is an ideal spot for surveying the
canyon's formations and colors. Other lookout points along the
rim include Hopi Point, Mohave Point, and Desert View.

Havasu Canyon is home to Arizona's three hundred Havasupai Indians.

U.S. Route 180 runs right up to Grand Canyon Village on the gorge's south rim. Visitors can also take a nostalgic, 64-mile (103-kilometer) train ride to the park on the Grand Canyon Railway from Williams. At the park entrance is the IMAX Theatre, showing a breathtaking, thirty-four-minute film called *Grand Canyon—The Hidden Secrets*.

There are many ways to enjoy the Grand Canyon. Some people hike the famous Bright Angel Trail down to the bottom of the canyon, arriving at Phantom Ranch lodge. Others take mule trips down into the canyon, raft on the Colorado River, or fly over the canyon in a helicopter or airplane from Grand Canyon Airport.

Farther west along the Colorado River is Havasu Canyon, the home of Arizona's three hundred Havasupai Indians. Their name means "people of the blue-green water," referring to the turquoise waters of beautiful Havasu Falls. On horse, on mule, or on foot, people can explore the canyon's red rock walls, streams, clear pools, peach tree stands, and magnificent waterfalls.

Williams, some 60 miles (97 kilometers) south of the Grand Canyon, was named for mountain man Bill Williams. The town's steam-powered Grand Canyon Railway, which ran from 1901 to 1968, has now been revived, complete with restored 1910 steam locomotives. Williams was the last town along old U.S. Route 66 to give way to Interstate 40. The day Route 66 closed, Bobby Troupe came to Williams and sang his famous song "Get Your Kicks on Route 66" to a nostalgic crowd.

Flagstaff, the largest city in northern Arizona, lies east of Williams along Interstate 40. On July 4, 1876, a flag was raised there on a tall ponderosa pine to celebrate the nation's centennial, giving the city its name. With an elevation of nearly 7,000 feet (2,134 meters), Flagstaff nestles in the foothills of the San Francisco Peaks, the state's tallest mountains. Just north of Flagstaff is Humphreys Peak, the state's highest point. The Flagstaff area is surrounded by the world's largest stand of ponderosa pines.

In downtown Flagstaff are a number of art galleries and shops that specialize in Indian jewelry. Visitors may browse in the Flagstaff Art Barn and the Pioneers' Historical Museum or enjoy an evening with the Flagstaff Symphony Orchestra.

Northern Arizona University (NAU) spreads over 700 acres (283 hectares) on the southwest side of town. Its thirteen thousand students have the benefit of a huge indoor sports facility, the NAU Skydome, as well as theater and art facilities.

On top of Mars Hill, west of downtown, is Lowell Observatory, founded by Percival Lowell in 1894. Visitors there can see the historic 24-inch (61-centimeter) Clark refractor telescope, through which Lowell made his observations of Mars. Here, too, Clyde

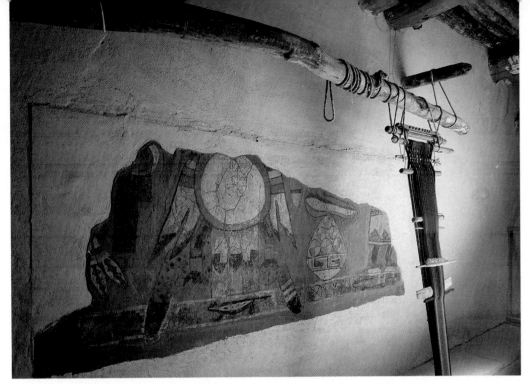

A reproduction of a Hopi mural adorns the wall of a full-sized replica of an Awatovi kiva at the Museum of Northern Arizona, just north of Flagstaff.

Tombaugh discovered the planet Pluto in 1930. Today, the observatory operates eight telescopes and maintains an active staff of astronomers.

The Museum of Northern Arizona, just north of town, is both a research center and a museum. Its exhibits illustrate northern Arizona's natural history, archaeology, and geology, as well as Navajo and Hopi culture. Farther north is Fairfield Snowbowl, a haven for alpine and cross-country skiers.

North of Flagstaff along U.S. Route 89 is Sunset Crater National Monument, where the giant black cinder cone of Arizona's last erupting volcano rises above the horizon. Lava flows, volcanic formations, and ice caves tell the tale of the eleventh-century eruption. Around the rim, minerals left by the volcano's vapors give off an eerie glow.

Farther north, Wupatki National Monument features several hundred Sinagua Indian dwellings. Dating from the twelfth

89

Diverse attractions at Sedona include the lovely display of luminarias at the Tlaquepaque shopping village during the annual Festival of Lights (left) and the spectacular Cathedral Rock formation at Oak Creek Canyon (right).

century, the Wupatki ruins range from one-family homes to a pueblo with more than one hundred rooms. Indians at Wupatki, a Hopi word meaning "tall house," farmed the rich volcanic ash left by Sunset Crater's eruption.

Just east of Flagstaff off Interstate 40 is Walnut Canyon National Monument. Sheltered under ledges in the limestone canyon's walls are ruins of more than three hundred Sinagua cliff dwellings, dating from about A.D. 1100.

About 35 miles (56 kilometers) east of Flagstaff is Meteor Crater, the best preserved meteor crater on earth. It was created nearly 50,000 years ago, when a huge meteor struck the earth at the speed of nearly 45,000 miles per hour (72,419 kilometers per hour). The impact left a hole 570 feet (174 meters) deep and nearly a mile (1.6 kilometers) across. Because the crater's dusty surface is much like the moon's, astronauts trained there for moon landings. Also at the site is the Astronaut Hall of Fame, displaying a real space capsule, and the Museum of Astrogeology.

An hour's drive east of Flagstaff is Winslow, originally named Brigham City by its Mormon settlers. Just outside of town is the site of the ancient Anasazi village of Homol'ovi, home of the Hopis' ancestors. Ruins of the village are now being excavated in Homol'ovi Ruins State Park, where visitors may watch the digs and examine petroglyphs, pottery shards, and other unearthed treasures.

South of Flagstaff, U.S. Route 89A drops steeply from the Colorado Plateau down the walls of Oak Creek Canyon. Over the years, Oak Creek has cut a 16-mile (26-kilometer) gorge through layers of sandstone, forming pools and rapids along the way. Rock formations in the canyon change color with the time of day and the seasons. In Slide Rock State Park, Oak Creek has worn a natural water slide on which visitors can slide downstream.

At the southern end of Oak Creek Canyon is Sedona, named in 1902 for Sedona Schnebly, the postmaster's wife. Sedona is a growing arts colony and home to many artists and celebrities. The resort town is full of gift shops and galleries with western and Indian art objects, sculptures, and paintings. Sedona's version of a shopping mall is Tlaquepaque (pronounced "T'lockapockay"), an Indian name meaning "the best of everything." Built in old Mexican style, the shopping complex is designed with gracious courtyards, tiled walkways, iron gates, and fountains.

Red Rock Crossing, west of Sedona, is a familiar sight. Hundreds of western movies and television shows have been filmed among its canyons and spectacular red rock formations.

This equestrian statue in front of
the Yavapai County Courthouse in
Prescott honors Spanish-American War
hero William O. "Bucky" O'Neil.

CENTRAL TERRITORY

Arizona's central territory is rich with history. Its ghost towns
tell of frontier boomtown days when fortunes were made from
and lost on the gold and copper in its hills. Overlooking the
territory are Indian dwellings from cultures that thrived hundreds
of years ago.

Prescott, named after historian William Hickling Prescott,
became Arizona's first territorial capital in 1864. Pine forests and
cool streams surround this high mountain town. Largely settled
by midwesterners, Prescott does not have the southwestern or
Mexican flavor of towns farther south. Prescott's Sharlot Hall
Museum is a group of historic buildings that includes the first

Cottonwoods line the Verde River near the town of Cottonwood.

Governor's Mansion and other old homes. Courthouse Plaza, in the center of town, is often the scene of dances, festivals, and fairs.

South of Prescott, in the foothills of the Bradshaw Mountains, is Wickenburg. Established by gold prospectors in 1864, Wickenburg now attracts vacationers who enjoy the area's dude ranches and resorts. Because old Wickenburg had no jail, prisoners were chained to the Jail Tree, a giant mesquite tree near the Hassayampa River.

North and east of Prescott is the valley of the Verde River. *Verde,* Spanish for "green," refers both to the green copper ore in rocks along the river and to the valley's lush vegetation. The towns of Cottonwood and Clarkdale are nestled high in the Verde Valley, while Camp Verde lies farther downstream.

Clinging to the side of Cleopatra Hill on Mingus Mountain is the old copper-mining town of Jerome. According to local legend, the famous Mexican revolutionary and bandit Pancho Villa hauled in the town's first water supply on the back of a mule. Once known as the "wickedest town in the West," Jerome grew to be one of Arizona's largest cities, with a population of fifteen thousand. After the copper mines closed in 1953, Jerome became almost a ghost town.

Now renovated and rebuilt, the whole town is a national historic landmark. Art galleries, antique stores, and renovated saloons line the streets. Jerome's old jailhouse is still standing, even though underground dynamite blasting in the 1920s moved it 225 feet (69 meters). In Jerome State Historic Park is the restored mansion of "Rawhide Jimmy" Douglas, one of Jerome's founders.

High on a ridgetop above the Verde River near Clarkdale is Tuzigoot National Monument. This prehistoric, 110-room Sinagua pueblo, which flourished from A.D. 1100 to 1450, was built on the ridge and terraced down the slopes. Today, visitors can take a walking tour of the ruins.

The road from Tuzigoot to Camp Verde drops steeply in a long stretch of hairpin curves. Near Camp Verde is Fort Verde State Historic Park. Established in 1865, the fort was the headquarters for cavalry troops fighting the Apaches in the 1870s and 1880s.

Montezuma Castle National Monument, a few miles north of Camp Verde, is a collection of Sinagua cliff dwellings built around A.D. 1250. Early settlers believed the ruins were left by Mexican Aztecs, whose emperor was named Montezuma. The "castle" itself—still 90 percent intact—is a five-story, twenty-room pueblo. Not far away is Montezuma Well, a limestone pit rimmed with cliff dwellings. From this pit, the Sinaguas channeled water to their farms below.

A Mogollon Rim scene

South of Camp Verde is Arcosanti, called the City of the Future. Architect Paolo Soleri designed the Arcosanti complex as a way of exploring new ways for people to live.

HIGH COUNTRY

East-central Arizona, called the high country, is a land of mountain lakes, cool pine forests, and abundant wildlife. In the region's White Mountains and national forests, visitors enjoy rappeling, backpacking, fishing, and cross-country skiing. The White Mountains rise atop the Mogollon Rim, a steep rock cliff between Arizona's high plateaus and southern lowlands.

Payson, in Tonto National Forest, is a base for adventurers heading into the surrounding area. Western novelist Zane Grey settled in a cabin northeast of Payson, where he wrote tales set in Arizona's mountains, forests, and canyons. Unfortunately, forest fires in the summer of 1990 destroyed the cabin.

Four Peaks, east
of Phoenix in Tonto
National Forest

Tonto Natural Bridge, also north of Payson, is the largest
travertine bridge in the world. Travertine bridges are formed by
mineral deposits from the waters of natural springs. Still fed by its
spring, the bridge stands 183 feet (56 meters) above Pine Creek on
the canyon floor.

The Fort Apache Indian Reservation, east of Payson, has a great
number of lakes and streams and includes a ski area. At the tribal
headquarters in Whiteriver, visitors can observe traditional
Apache ceremonies. Many original buildings still stand at nearby
Theodore Roosevelt Indian School. The museum on the school's
grounds includes historic old Fort Apache, a famous military post
during the Apache wars.

The mountain towns of Pinetop, Lakeside, and Show Low line
the Mogollon Rim. In 1876, two ranchers wanted the same range
and drew cards to decide who would get it. "Show low and you
win," one of them said. The other drew the deuce (two) of clubs

A cowboy bursts out
of the chute at the
White Mountain Apache
Rodeo in Whiteriver,
on the Fort Apache
Indian Reservation.

and took the range, called Show Low ever since. Now, Show
Low's main street is named Deuce of Clubs. The town is a center
for the White Mountain Recreation Area, a haven for fishing,
hunting, camping, skiing, horseback riding, canoeing, and sailing.

U.S. Route 666 winds through 125 miles (201 kilometers) of
mountains in the Apache-Sitgreaves National Forest along
Arizona's eastern edge. Called the Coronado Trail, it roughly
follows the trail of the Spanish conquistador on his quest for the
Seven Cities of Cibola.

South of Salt River Canyon, the dividing line between the Fort
Apache and San Carlos Indian reservations, are Miami and Globe,
two more of Arizona's historic mining towns. Globe is the eastern
endpoint of the Apache Trail, now Arizona 88 between Globe and
Phoenix. Apache Indians once took this scenic mountain trail
through the Superstition Mountains. Legend has it that
somewhere in these mountains, near a rock spire called Weaver's

Theodore Roosevelt Dam is located on the Salt River along the Apache Trail.

Needle, is the Lost Dutchman Mine. The exact location of this gold mine is one of the great mysteries of the Southwest.

Along the Salt River are dams creating Saguaro, Canyon, Apache, and Theodore Roosevelt lakes. Theodore Roosevelt Dam stands 275 feet (84 meters) high and forms a lake 25 miles (40 kilometers) long. When Roosevelt himself spoke at the dam's dedication in 1911, he called the area "the most awe-inspiring and most sublimely beautiful panorama nature has ever created." Just east of Roosevelt Dam is Tonto National Monument. Its well-preserved Salado Indian cliff dwellings were built some six hundred years ago.

THE GOLDEN CORRIDOR

Arizona's Golden Corridor stretches from Phoenix to Tucson, the state's two metropolitan areas. Phoenix, the state capital, lies in a basin in the Salt River Valley. Clustered around it are several

Phoenix
★

● Coolidge

Arizona-Sonora
Desert Museum ▲   ▲ Mount Lemmon
Kitt Peak ●   ● Tuscon
National
Observatory   ● San Xavier

The business-area skyline of Tucson

communities, including Sun City, Glendale, Scottsdale, Mesa, Tempe, and Chandler. Altogether, they make up what is called the Valley of the Sun. The name fits, as the valley enjoys an average of 306 days of sunshine a year. Visitors from all over the country come to the Valley of the Sun for its resorts, golf courses, and dude ranches. With more than one hundred thousand newcomers every year, it is the fastest growing area in the country.

Phoenix is the nation's ninth-largest city. Orange and grapefruit trees flourish in downtown Phoenix, and palm trees line major thoroughfares. The modern Civic Plaza includes a concert hall and convention center. In contrast, nearby Heritage Square is a full city block of restored historic buildings from the 1800s. Across from Civic Plaza, visitors can explore the world of science in the Arizona Museum of Science and Technology.

At the head of Washington Street is Arizona's state capitol, crowned by the winged figure of Victory. Inside is the State Capitol Museum. Throughout the building are colorful murals

Rosson House, a carefully restored 1895 Victorian-style mansion, dominates Heritage Square in Phoenix (left). Phoenix's Heard Museum of Anthropology and Primitive Art (right) has one of the finest collections of Indian artifacts in the world.

and paintings depicting Arizona's historic events and scenic landscapes.

On Central Avenue is the Central Arizona Museum of History, housing an old-time drugstore, a costume gallery, and an exhibit on Arizona's ostrich-raising days. Just to the north is the Phoenix Art Museum, with paintings, sculptures, and other art from the fifteenth century to the present.

Farther north is the Heard Museum of Anthropology and Primitive Art, one of the finest collections of Indian artifacts in the world. Both prehistoric and modern-day southwestern Indian cultures are represented by thousands of artifacts. One room is filled with the kachina collection of former Arizona senator Barry Goldwater. In a special children's area, visitors can make corn-husk dolls and hear Indian legends.

On the east side of Phoenix is Pueblo Grande, a prehistoric Hohokam settlement occupied from about 200 B.C. to A.D. 1450.

Besides the ruins of Hohokam canals, there is a museum with displays of artifacts excavated from the site.

Farther east, in Papago Park, is the Desert Botanical Garden. This outdoor museum displays more than ten thousand varieties of cactus and other plants from deserts all over the world. Jackrabbits, squirrels, desert tortoises, and other creatures creep and scurry through the natural desert habitat. In one area, children may grind corn and mesquite beans and make yucca brushes. Cactus lovers may want to stop for the garden's occasional plant sales, since taking a cactus from the desert is against state law.

Next to the garden is the Phoenix Zoo, which includes a children's zoo. Other interesting spots in Phoenix are the Hall of Flame fire-fighting museum and the Arizona Mineral Museum with collections of petrified wood and gemstones.

Directly east of Phoenix is Scottsdale, the old homestead of army chaplain Winfield Scott. Known as an artists' center, Scottsdale is full of galleries and boutiques. The 20-acre (8-hectare) Scottsdale Mall is the largest in the country. To the north, in the foothills of the McDowell Mountains, is Taliesin West, the desert home, studio, and architecture school of Frank Lloyd Wright.

South of Scottsdale is Tempe, Arizona's fifth-largest city and the home of Arizona State University. The campus's Gammage Center for the Performing Arts was one of Frank Lloyd Wright's last designs. Near the university are the quaint shops of Old Town Tempe. In the Salt River Project History Center, artifacts and video presentations take visitors through the valley's irrigation history.

East of Tempe is Mesa, the third-largest city in the state. Hotels, shopping centers, and high-tech industries have all contributed to

Mesa's growth. Reconstructions of a Hohokam pit house and a Salado cliff house await visitors to the Mesa Southwest Museum. North of Mesa, the Park of the Canals is the only place where visitors can trace ancient Hohokam canals, see remnants of Phoenix's pioneers' canals, and watch a modern Salt River Project canal all at once.

From the Valley of the Sun, people may take jeep tours of the Sonoran Desert while guides tell of the area's history and legends. South Mountain Park, south of Phoenix, is the largest city park in the world. Visitors can see a spectacular view of the valley from an elevation of 1,000 feet (305 meters).

In Coolidge, about halfway between Phoenix and Tucson, is Casa Grande Ruins National Monument. A mysterious, mud-walled tower is the major attraction in this eight-hundred-year-old Hohokam settlement. Mount Lemmon, northeast of Tucson, is the southernmost ski area in the country. In Sabino Canyon, south of Mount Lemmon, are streams, waterfalls, hiking trails, and a wildlife refuge.

Tucson, once the capital of the Arizona Territory, lies in a desert valley surrounded by the Santa Catalina, Sierrita, Santa Rita, and Rincon mountain ranges. Known as the Old Pueblo, it served under Spanish, Mexican, Confederate, and United States flags. It is also one of the oldest continuously inhabited places in the country. A walk through some of Tucson's historic areas provides a glimpse into the past.

The modern Tucson Museum of Art in El Presidio shares grounds with four historic adobe homes. Old Town Artisans is a collection of shops housed in historic buildings.

The campus of the University of Arizona houses the Arizona State Museum, the Center for Creative Photography, the Museum of Art, the Mineralogical Museum, and the Grace H. Flandrau

San Xavier del Bac Mission (left), south of Tucson, is called the White Dove of the Desert. The Kitt Peak Observatory (above), also south of Tucson, is a large facility for stellar and solar research.

Planetarium. Eighteen buildings on campus are listed in the National Register of Historic Places. On the northeast side of Tucson is Fort Lowell Park and Museum, the main army base during the Apache wars.

Just outside of Tucson, there is even more to see. To the west is the famous movie set of Old Tucson. Built as a backdrop for the 1939 film classic *Arizona*, it has been the setting for more than one hundred movies and countless television shows and commercials. Now Old Tucson is an Old West theme park.

Farther west, the Arizona-Sonora Desert Museum covers 12 acres (5 hectares) with fascinating displays. The museum complex includes a botanical garden, a mineral collection, an aquarium, and a zoo where animals roam around in their natural habitat.

South of Tucson rise the gleaming white towers of San Xavier del Bac Mission, called the White Dove of the Desert. It is one of the

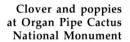

**Clover and poppies
at Organ Pipe Cactus
National Monument**

oldest churches in the country that is still being used. Today, it is
the house of worship for Tohono O'odham Indians of the San
Xavier Reservation. Visitors may enter the church every day
except Sunday, when masses are held. Kitt Peak National
Observatory, southwest of the mission, is the world's largest
facility for stellar and solar research.

Both east and west of Tucson is Saguaro National Monument, a
thick forest of giant saguaro cactus plants. Hiking trails wind
through this desert valley for those who wish to view the huge
saguaros at close range.

OLD WEST COUNTRY

Arizona's southeast corner is a land of high desert valleys and
evergreen-forested mountains. Here, too, lurk many legends of the
Old West.

104

The old Spanish presidio of Tubac, Arizona's oldest continuously inhabited European settlement, is now a haven for artists and craftspeople. At nearby Tumacacori National Monument are the ruins of the Franciscan mission church founded by Padre Kino.

From Nogales, at the Mexican border, travelers can stroll across to its Mexican "twin city" of Nogales, Sonora. Shoppers find fabulous bargains in Mexican Nogales, an international free port. Handcrafted Mexican goods are available, as well as items from other countries.

Northwest of Nogales, beyond the Papago Indian Reservation, is Organ Pipe Cactus National Monument. This is the only place in the world where this type of cactus grows.

East of Nogales, at Sierra Vista, is Fort Huachuca. The country's only remaining active cavalry post, the fort is now the Army Information Systems Command and Electronic Proving Ground. On the base is Fort Huachuca Historical Museum, with exhibits from the days of the Apache wars to the present. Near Sierra Vista is Ramsey Canyon Preserve, a famous sanctuary for fourteen species of hummingbirds, as well as other wildlife.

A few miles northeast of Sierra Vista is Tombstone, the "town too tough to die." Tombstone was once one of the most sophisticated, cultured cities in the West. Still preserved there are sites such as the OK Corral, where lawman Wyatt Earp had one of the old West's most famous shootouts. In Boothill Cemetery lie such legendary figures as Tom and Frank McLaury and Billy Clanton, victims of the gunfight at OK Corral.

The old mining town of Bisbee, in the Mule Mountains south of Tombstone, is now home to many artists and craftspeople. Bisbee is the site of the awesome Lavender Pit Copper Mine, as well as Brewery Gulch, a famous strip of saloons and gambling houses. At the nearby Copper Queen Mine, where miners are the guides, visitors don mining gear and descend into the mine.

In the southeast corner of the state is Douglas. Many people cross over the border to visit Mexico from here. Douglas's pride is its extravagant five-story Gadsden Hotel, built in 1907 and renovated to its original grandeur. President Theodore Roosevelt was one of the distinguished guests in this landmark hotel.

RIVER COUNTRY

Arizona's western edge, from Hoover Dam on the north to Mexico on the south, is formed by 340 miles (547 kilometers) of Colorado River shore. This long stretch of sandy beaches and high ridges is ideal for sailing, boating, fishing, sailboarding, and white-water rafting.

Behind Hoover Dam is massive Lake Mead, the largest artificially made lake in the United States. Measuring 115 miles (185 kilometers) long, Lake Mead is dotted with pleasure boats and houseboats.

Lake Mohave, south of Hoover Dam, is formed by Davis Dam. A fisherman at nearby Bullhead City caught the largest striped bass ever found in an inland waterway. The monster bass weighed in at 59 pounds, 12 ounces (27 kilograms). In Grapevine Canyon near Bullhead City is Christmas Tree Pass, where prehistoric petroglyphs tell stories of ancient hunts.

East of Bullhead City is Kingman, whose Mohave Museum of History and Art exhibits a collection of carved turquoise. Southwest of there is the old gold-mining town of Oatman. From 1900 to 1930, over $30 million worth of gold came from the area's mines. Now, Oatman is a ghost town, where wild burros wander the streets hoping to munch on food from visitors' hands.

The dedication ceremony of London Bridge at Lake Havasu City

Farther south is Lake Havasu City, whose major attraction is the 952-foot (290-meter) London Bridge. The bridge was dismantled and brought over from England in 1968, and it took until 1971 to reconstruct it piece by piece. Lake Havasu City sits on the shores of Lake Havasu, created by Parker Dam.

In Yuma is the Century House Museum, the Arizona Historical Society's museum for the region, with exhibits about the Indians, explorers, miners, riverboat captains, and settlers of the area. The infamous Yuma Territorial Prison, built by convicts in 1875, stands on Prison Hill.

From deserts to mountain forests to high plateaus, Arizona dares the adventurous, bewitches the curious, and charms the simple heart.

FACTS AT A GLANCE

GENERAL INFORMATION

Statehood: February 14, 1912, forty-eighth state

Origin of Name: Most scholars believe the name Arizona comes from the Tohono O'odham (Papago) Indian word *arizonac*, meaning "small spring." Another theory suggests that the name comes from the Aztec word *arizuma*, meaning "silver-bearing."

State Capital: Phoenix, founded 1867

State Nickname: Arizona's official nickname is Grand Canyon State. Its other nicknames are Valentine State, because Arizona became a state on Valentine's Day; and Baby State, because Arizona was the nation's youngest state for forty-seven years.

State Flag: Arizona adopted the design for its state flag in 1917. In the center of the flag is a five-pointed, copper-colored star, representing the state's most valuable mineral. The lower half of the background is a field of blue. Radiating upward from the star to represent an Arizona sunset are thirteen rays, alternating red and yellow. These are the colors of Arizona's historic Spanish explorers.

State Motto: *Ditat Deus*, "God Enriches"

State Bird: Cactus wren

State Flower: Saguaro cactus blossom

State Tree: Paloverde

State Mammal: Ring-tailed cat

State Reptile: Ridge-nosed rattlesnake

State Gemstone: Turquoise

State Fossil: Petrified wood

State Neckwear: Bola tie, which originated in Arizona

State Song: "Arizona March Song," words by Margaret Rowe Clifford and music by Maurice Blumenthal, adopted as the state song in 1919:

Come to this land of sunshine
To this land where life is young.
Where the wide, wide world is waiting,
The songs that will now be sung.
Where the golden sun is flaming
Into warm, white, shining day,
And the sons of men are blazing
Their priceless right of way.

Chorus:
Sing the song that's in your hearts
Sing of the great Southwest,
Thank God, for Arizona
In splendid sunshine dressed.
For thy beauty and thy grandeur,
For thy regal robes so sheen
We hail thee Arizona
Our Goddess and our queen.

Come stand beside the rivers
Within our valleys broad.
Stand here with heads uncovered,
In the presence of our God!
While all around, about us
The brave, unconquered band,
As guardians and landmarks
The giant mountains stand.

Chorus

Not alone for gold and silver
Is Arizona great.
But with graves of heroes sleeping,
All the land is consecrate!
O, come and live beside us
However far ye roam
Come help us build up temples
And name those temples "home."

In 1982, Arizona's legislature adopted "Arizona," with words and music by Rex Allen, Jr., as the alternate state song:

I love you, Arizona
Your mountains, deserts and streams
The rise of Dos Cabezas
And the outlaws I see in my dreams.

I love you Arizona
Superstitions and all
The warmth you give at sunrise
Your sunsets put music in us all.

Chorus:
Oo, Arizona
You're the magic in me
Oo, Arizona
You're the life-blood of me.

I love you Arizona
Desert dust on the wind
The sage and cactus are blooming
And the smell of the rain on your skin.

Chorus

POPULATION

Population: 2,718,425, twenty-ninth among the states (1980 census; the 1989 population estimate of 3,600,000 places Arizona twenty-fifth among the states)

Population Density: 24 persons per sq. mi. (9 persons per km²)

Population Distribution: Eighty-four percent of Arizona's people live in cities or towns. Phoenix, the state capital, is the largest city. Three-fourths of Arizona's residents live in the Phoenix and Tucson metropolitan areas.

Phoenix	789,704
Tucson	330,537
Mesa	152,453
Tempe	106,920
Glendale	97,172
Scottsdale	88,622
Yuma	42,481
Flagstaff	34,743
Chandler	29,673
Sierra Vista	24,937

(Population figures according to 1980 census)

Population Growth: In the 1970s, Arizona's population grew more than 53 percent, while the overall population of the United States rose only 11.4 percent. Only the state of Nevada experienced a more rapid growth in the 1970s.

Year	Population
1870	9,658
1880	40,440
1890	88,243
1900	122,931
1920	334,162
1940	499,261
1950	749,587
1960	1,302,161
1970	1,775,399
1980	2,718,425

GEOGRAPHY

Borders: Arizona is bordered by Utah on the north, New Mexico on the east, and the Mexican state of Sonora on the south. Nevada and California border Arizona on the west. Colorado touches Arizona's northeast corner, where the states of Utah, Colorado, New Mexico, and Arizona meet at right angles at a point known as Four Corners.

Rainbow Bridge, at Lake Powell

Highest Point: Humphreys Peak, 12,633 ft. (3,851 m)

Lowest Point: Yuma County, along the Colorado River, 70 ft. (21 m) above sea level

Greatest Distances: North to south—389 mi. (626 km)
East to west—337 mi. (542 km)

Area: 114,000 sq. mi. (295,260 km²)

Rank in Area Among the States: Sixth

National Forests and Parklands: Arizona has twenty national parklands, seven national forests, and twenty-one state parks. The National Park Service administers Canyon de Chelly, Casa Grande Ruins, Chiricahua, Montezuma Castle, Navajo, Organ Pipe Cactus, Pipe Spring, Saguaro, Sunset Crater, Tonto, Tumacacori, Tuzigoot, Walnut Canyon, and Wupatki national monuments. Other National Park Service lands are Glen Canyon and Lake Mead national recreation areas, Fort Bowie and Hubbell Trading Post national historic sites, Coronado National Memorial, and Grand Canyon and Petrified Forest national parks. Arizona's national forests cover about 11.3 million acres (4.6 million hectares). Administered by the U.S. Department of Agriculture Forest Service, they include Apache, Coconino, Coronado, Kaibab, Prescott, Sitgreaves, and Tonto national forests.

Rivers: The Colorado River is Arizona's most important river, flowing through the state for 688 mi. (1,107 km). From Utah, the Colorado enters Arizona at the center of its northern border. It flows south and then west for 277 mi. (446 km), with most of this course through the Grand Canyon. Turning southward, it then forms Arizona's border with Nevada and California. Along with its tributaries, the Colorado river system drains more than 90 percent of the state's land area. Its major tributaries are the Gila, which joins the Colorado at Yuma; the Little Colorado, which branches off at the Grand Canyon; and the Bill Williams, which flows into the Colorado near Parker Dam. The Salt River, flowing past Phoenix, provides irrigation water for much of central Arizona.

On the surface, most of Arizona's smaller streams dry up during the summer, although underground water continues to flow beneath them. Mountain streams plunging down into the Grand Canyon create many beautiful waterfalls, including Bridal Veil Falls, Havasu Falls, Beaver Falls, Navajo Falls, and Mooney Falls.

Lakes: Arizona has few natural lakes. However, a number of large artificial lakes have been created by building dams along the state's rivers and streams. The largest lakes lie along the Colorado, Gila, and Salt rivers. Along the Colorado River, Glen Canyon Dam buttresses Lake Powell, Hoover Dam holds Lake Mead, Davis Dam supports Lake Mohave, and Parker Dam is backed by Havasu Lake. On the Gila River, Carlos Lake backs Coolidge Dam. Dams along the Salt River form Theodore Roosevelt, Canyon, Saguaro, and Apache lakes.

Topography: Arizona's elevation generally slopes from northeast to southwest. The state's three major land regions are the Colorado Plateau, the mountain zone, and the desert region. The Colorado Plateau covers the northern and northeastern portions of Arizona and extends into Utah, Colorado, and New Mexico. High plateaus, flat-topped mesas, deep canyons, and volcanoes' craters are characteristic of the Colorado Plateau. Deserts, hardwood forests, and snow-covered slopes are all found in the Colorado Plateau. In the northwestern part of Arizona, the Colorado River has formed the Grand Canyon, the longest and deepest canyon in the state. Tributaries of the Colorado River have formed other canyons in the plateau, including Canyon de Chelly and Oak Creek Canyon. North of the Colorado River is an area called the Arizona Strip. Here, from west to east, rise the Shivwits, Kanab, Kaibab, and Paria plateaus. The Little Colorado River bends around Arizona's northeast corner, enclosing the Kaibito Plateau; the Black Mesa, with its three fingerlike extensions; the Painted Desert, with its prehistoric forest of petrified wood; Defiance Plateau; and Canyon de Chelly. A group of strange rock formations at the Arizona-Utah border is known as Monument Valley. The southern part of the Colorado Plateau, south of the Colorado River, is called the San Francisco Plateau. This region has a lower elevation than the land to the north. Among the San Francisco Peaks, however, is 12,633-ft. (3,851-m) Humphreys Peak, the highest point in the state.

South of the Colorado Plateau is the mountain zone, or Transition Zone, between the high plateaus and the desert. This northwest-to-southeast strip of land includes the Mazatzal, Santa Maria, Sierra Ancha, and White mountain ranges. A steep-walled ridge called the Mogollon Rim, which continues east into New Mexico, runs across the northern part of the region. Along with the plains to the south, this zone is often classified as part of North America's Mexican Highland Region.

Arizona's low desert region, or Basin and Range region, covers roughly the southwestern half of the state and extends along the state's western border and widens to the southwest and the south. The Sonoran Desert covers the large central portion of this region. Throughout the desert plains rise several low, heavily forested mountain ranges, including the Harcuvar, Castle Dome, Gila, Gila Bend, Sand Tank, Ajo, Baboquivari, Santa Catalina, Santa Rita, Pinaleno, Galiuro, and Chiricahua mountains. The Gila River and its major tributary, the Salt River, bring moisture to the Sonoran Desert region.

Climate: Arizona enjoys generally clear skies and dry air. The dry air makes temperature extremes less uncomfortable. There are great differences in climate between the cooler mountainous northern parts of the state and the warmer desert area in the south. The highest temperature ever recorded in Arizona was 127° F. (53° C) in Parker on July 7, 1905. The record low was -40° F. (-40° C) at Hawley Lake on January 7, 1971. Statewide, the average temperature in July is 80° F. (27° C), and the January average is 41° F. (5° C).

The state's precipitation, or moisture such as rain and snow, also varies greatly from one part of the state to another. Desert areas average 3 in. (8 cm) of precipitation a year, while the White Mountains can receive as much as 30 in. (76 cm) per year. Statewide, the average annual precipitation is 13 in. (33 cm).

NATURE

Trees: Quaking aspens, Douglas firs, white firs, subalpine firs, cork bark firs, birches, piñon pines, ponderosa pines, bristlecone pines, blue spruces, Englemann spruces, oaks, sycamores, cherry, walnut, paloverde, Joshua, junipers, cottonwoods, palms, oaks, Gambel oaks, olives

Wild Plants: Cactus (cholla, prickly pear, barrel, organ-pipe, saguaro), creosote, ocotillo, mesquite, manzanita, ironwood, cereus, yucca, geraniums, columbines, paint brushes, phlox, pinks, poppies, groundsels, buttercups, sand verbenas

Animals: Mule deer, white-tailed deer, pronghorn antelopes, brown bears, black bears, elks, mountain sheep, desert bighorn sheep, lynxes, bobcats, mountain lions, ocelots, coatis, badgers, beavers, red foxes, kit foxes, coyotes, raccoons, otters, skunks, porcupines, cottontail rabbits, jackrabbits, chipmunks, squirrels, Kaibab squirrels, weasels, pocket gophers, mice, kangaroo rats, javelinas, lizards, Gila monsters, diamondback rattlesnakes, garter snakes, gopher snakes, hognosed snakes, coral snakes, scorpions, tarantulas, black widow spiders, centipedes

Birds: Cactus wrens, doves, grouse, Gambel's quails, Gila woodpeckers, Steller's jays, roadrunners, hawks, eagles, owls, ravens, hummingbirds, juncos, wild turkeys

Fish: Trout, bass, bluegills, crappies

GOVERNMENT

Arizona's state government, like the federal government, is divided into legislative, executive, and judicial branches. The legislature, which makes state laws, is composed of a thirty-member senate and a sixty-member house of representatives. The legislators are elected from thirty legislative districts, each of which elects one senator and two representatives. All legislators serve two-year terms.

Arizona's governor, as the chief executive, enforces the state's laws. There is no lieutenant governor; an unexpected vacancy in the governorship is filled by another executive officer, in the following order of succession: secretary of state, attorney general, state treasurer, and superintendent of public instruction. The governor and other executive officials are elected to four-year terms and may be reelected any number of times, with the exception of the state treasurer, who can serve for no more than three consecutive terms.

Arizona's state supreme court heads the judicial branch, which interprets the laws. The Commission on Appellate Court Appointments nominates candidates for supreme court seats, and the governor appoints five justices from that list. Those justices then elect one of their members as chief justice. Supreme court justices serve six-year terms, after which the people vote on whether to retain each judge. The second-highest court is the court of appeals, with twelve judges serving in the Phoenix division and three judges serving in the Tucson division. These judges are selected and serve in the same way as the supreme court justices. Major civil and criminal cases are heard by superior court judges in each county. Justices of the peace and municipal court judges hear minor cases.

Each of Arizona's fifteen counties is governed by a three-person board of supervisors, who serve for two-year terms. Other county officers include the sheriff, the county attorney, and the assessor. The county governs unincorporated cities and towns. Of those that are incorporated, the larger cities and towns are directed by a city manager, who reports to the city council. Smaller towns elect a five- to seven-member council, which chooses one of its members to be the mayor. Cities and towns may also apply to the state legislature to receive a home-rule charter.

Number of Counties: 15

U.S. Representatives: 5

Electoral Votes: 7

Voting Qualifications: Eighteen years of age; one year state residency; thirty days county and district residency

EDUCATION

Seventy-two percent of Arizonans over the age of twenty-four have earned high-school diplomas, while the country as a whole averages only 67 percent. College

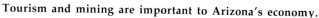
Tourism and mining are important to Arizona's economy.

graduates make up 17 percent of Arizona's population, slightly more than the national average of 16 percent.

Children in Arizona are required to attend school between the ages of eight and sixteen. About 595,000 students attend Arizona's public schools. The public school system offers special programs for gifted, learning-disabled, and handicapped students.

Arizona has nine accredited colleges and universities. Those located in Phoenix are the University of Phoenix, Western International University, Grand Canyon University, and DeVry Institute of Technology. Tucson is the home of the University of Arizona. Others are Northern Arizona University in Flagstaff, Arizona State University in Tempe, Prescott College in Prescott, and the American Graduate School of International Management Thunderbird Campus in Glendale. Navajo Community College in Tsaile, founded in 1969, was the nation's first institution of higher learning to open on an Indian reservation.

ECONOMY AND INDUSTRY

Principal Products:

Agriculture: Beef cattle, cotton, cottonseed, milk and other dairy products, hay, lettuce, sorghum grain, barley, corn, potatoes, wheat, poultry, eggs, sheep, lambs, Angora goats, citrus fruit, nursery products, grapes, honey

Manufacturing: Electrical and nonelectrical machinery, transportation equipment, food products, fabricated metal products, primary metals, electronic equipment, computers, instruments, aerospace equipment, printed materials, stone and clay products, glass products

Natural Resources: Copper, silver, zinc, gold, lead, uranium, vanadium, molybdenum, manganese, tungsten, mercury, coal, petroleum, natural gas, helium, sand and gravel, stone, asbestos, lime gypsum, feldspar, quartz, pumice, diatomite, perlite, pyrite, mica, clay, bentonite, iron, salt, timber

Business: The service industry—which includes tourism-related services— employs about 360,000 people, making it Arizona's largest employer. The wholesale and retail trades are a close second, with more than 350,000 employees. Manufacturing accounts for 16 percent of the gross state product, with electrical machinery and equipment, nonelectrical machinery, and transportation equipment as the leading industries. Since the 1970s, many high-technology companies have located in Arizona, manufacturing computers, electronic components, and aerospace equipment. Mining and agriculture remain important segments of Arizona's economy. With more than 20 million tourists visiting Arizona each year, the tourist industry generates $5 billion to $6 billion annually.

Communication: The Arizona Territory's first newspaper, the *Weekly Arizonian*, was first published in Tubac in 1859. Now, about sixty weekly newspapers and a dozen daily newspapers are published in the state. Phoenix's *Arizona Republic* and *Gazette* and Tucson's *Arizona Daily Star* and *Citizen* have the largest circulations. *Arizona Highways*, a magazine published by the state highway department, is well known for its color illustrations. About ninety radio stations and seventeen commercial and educational television stations broadcast throughout the state. Arizona's first commercial radio station was Phoenix's KTAR, which began operation in 1922. Phoenix's KPHO-TV, the state's first television station, opened in 1949.

Transportation: Arizona's early stagecoach lines, the "Jackass Mail" and the Butterfield Overland Mail, provided passenger service across the territory before railroads were built. In 1877, the Southern Pacific Railroad began operation through southern Arizona, extending service to Phoenix in 1887. The Atlantic and Pacific Railroad, part of a transcontinental rail route, began running through northern Arizona in 1883. Today, railroads operate on about 1,600 mi. (2,575 km) of track in Arizona, most of them providing freight service. Arizona's 77,000 mi. (123,916 km) of paved roadways include Interstate 17, the state's major north-south route, and Interstates 8, 10, and 40, which run east and west. Interstate 40 replaced the legendary U.S. Route 66. Tucson was the first city in the country to have its own city airport, which was built in 1919. Now Sky Harbor International Airport in Phoenix is the state's busiest airport. About two hundred airports operate throughout the state. Eighteen major airlines provide service to Arizona.

SOCIAL AND CULTURAL LIFE

Museums: Arizona has more than one hundred museums that showcase the state's native heritage, western lore, natural history, arts, and culture. The Phoenix Art Museum houses an extensive visual arts collection and also presents special exhibits and educational programs. Pre-Columbian, western, and American art are featured in the Tucson Museum of Art. Phoenix's Heard Museum of Anthropology and Primitive Art has one of the finest collections of Native American artifacts in the world. Both a museum and a research center, the Museum of Northern Arizona in Flagstaff features exhibits on the art, anthropology, and geology of Arizona's northern plateau region. Mesa's Arizona Museum for Youth offers hands-on fine-arts demonstrations and projects for young people. Both the University of Arizona in Tucson and Arizona State University in Tempe maintain their own art museums. Also at the University of Arizona is the Center for Creative Photography, an archive of twentieth-century photographers' works. Many of Arizona's Indian reservations operate museums featuring Native American art and cultural artifacts. These include the Apache Culture Center at Fort Apache, the Colorado River Indian Tribal Museum in Parker, the Gila River Arts and Crafts Center in Sacaton, the Hopi Cultural Center on Second Mesa, the Navajo Tribal Museum in Window Rock, and Pueblo Grande Museum in Phoenix.

Libraries: By the 1870s, the towns of Phoenix, Tucson, and Prescott had opened small libraries. The Arizona Territorial Library, established in 1864, eventually became Arizona's present-day department of libraries and archives. Today, that department maintains about 160 public library facilities throughout Arizona. Its bookmobiles bring library services to many remote areas of the state. The University of Arizona in Tucson boasts the state's largest library, and Arizona State University in Tempe houses the second-largest one.

Performing Arts: Arizona's performing artists offer music, theater, and dance for all tastes. The Phoenix Symphony Orchestra is Arizona's major orchestra. Other fine orchestras in the state are the Tucson Symphony Orchestra and the Flagstaff Symphony Orchestra. The Mesa Symphony Orchestra, Scottsdale Symphony, Sun Cities Symphony Orchestra, and Tucson Pops Orchestra also offer their communities a season of orchestral fare. Many of Arizona's chamber music ensembles feature highly acclaimed guest soloists. Chamber music presenters in the state include the Phoenix Chamber Music Society, the Sun City Fine Arts Society, the Ethington Chamber Music Series of Phoenix, Arizona Friends of Music in Tucson, Scottsdale's Nouveau West Chamber Orchestra, the Sedona Chamber Music Society, and the Grand Canyon Chamber Music Festival. Music lovers also enjoy concerts by Tucson's Arizona Early Music Society and the Phoenix Early Music Society. The Arizona Opera Company, the only professional opera company in the state, presents opera seasons in both Phoenix and Tucson.

About ninety professional and community theater groups are active in Arizona. The Arizona Theatre Company, the state's only resident professional drama group, takes to the stage in both Phoenix and Tucson. Smaller professional companies include Actors Lab Arizona in Scottsdale and Actors Theatre of Phoenix. Phoenix's Musical Theatre of Arizona brings in guest artists to perform with local professionals. The Phoenix Little Theatre is the country's oldest community theater company. Tucson's Invisible Theatre supplements its regular season with projects for the elderly, the handicapped, and juvenile offenders. Tempe's Childsplay, Inc., gives award-winning performances for young people. Phoenix's Black Theatre Troupe highlights black literature, features local black actors, and trains young black performers. Arizona's Spanish-language and Spanish/English theater companies include Teatro Carmen, Borderlands Theatre, and Teatro el Sol, in Tucson; and Chicanos por la Causa, in Phoenix.

Folklorico de Guadalupano Dancers performing at Tlaquepaque during an annual festival

Classical, modern, and ethnic dance troupes perform in Arizona. Phoenix's Ballet Arizona, the Yuma Ballet Theatre and Performing Arts Company, and Tucson's Ballet Arts Foundation offer classical ballet. Modern dance companies include the Center Dance Ensemble of Phoenix, Desert Dance Theatre of Tempe, Orts Theatre of Dance and Tenth Street Danceworks of Tucson, and Intimate Flight Dance Company of Flagstaff. Flamenco is the specialty of Tucson's Aires Flamencos and Phoenix's Artes Bellas. Other ethnic ensembles include Phoenix's Kawambe African Drum and Dance Ensemble, Laura Moya Institute of Hispanic Dance, and Primavera; and Tucson's Barbara Williams Performing Arts Company and Ballet Folklorico Mexicana.

Sports and Recreation: Arizona's twenty national parklands, seven national forests, and twenty-one state parks draw sightseers, hikers, backpackers, campers, boaters, fishers, and hunters, as well as history, archaeology, and geology buffs. Drawing more than four million tourists a year, Grand Canyon National Park is one of the most-visited national parks in the country. Arizona's state parks are classified into four categories: water-based parks, desert parks, historic parks, and educational parks.

Arizona hosts professional football, basketball, hockey, baseball, golf, and tennis. The state gained its first professional football team, the Phoenix Cardinals, in 1988. The Cardinals, formerly of St. Louis, Missouri, belong to the eastern division of the national conference of the National Football League (NFL). They train in Flagstaff and play home games in Tempe's Sun Devil Stadium. The Phoenix Suns are members of the National Basketball Association and play in the Pacific division of the western conference. Both the Suns and the Phoenix Roadrunners, a professional hockey team, play home games in the Arizona Veterans' Memorial Coliseum in Phoenix. Eight major-league baseball teams, called the Cactus League, hold spring training in Arizona. In the American League, the Cleveland Indians train in Tucson, the Milwaukee Brewers in Chandler, the Seattle Mariners in Tempe, the California Angels in Mesa, and the Oakland Athletics in Phoenix. In the National League, the San Francisco Giants train in Scottsdale, the Chicago Cubs in Mesa, and the San Diego Padres in Yuma. Arizona's golf courses are regularly on the circuits of the Professional Golf Association and the Ladies Professional Golf Association, and the state often hosts professional tennis tours. Amateur and semiprofessional golfers also enjoy Arizona's many golf courses. The state claims to have more golf courses than any other state in the country.

Historic Sites and Landmarks:

Coronado National Memorial, south of Sierra Vista on the Arizona-Mexico border, is an area traversed by Francisco de Coronado while searching for the Seven Cities of Cibola.

Fort Bowie National Historic Site, south of Willcox, was a center for the army's resistance against Geronimo and the Chiricahua Apaches.

Hubbell Trading Post National Historic Site, in Ganado, includes the Navajo trading post established by John Lorenzo Hubbell in the 1870s and Hubbell's house, decorated with his Navajo rugs and other artifacts.

Jerome State Historic Park, in Jerome, features James "Rawhide Jimmy" Douglas's 1917 mansion and other buildings from the height of the town's copper-mining days.

Painted Rocks State Historic Park, near Gila Bend, contains boulders with prehistoric Indian petroglyphs, or rock drawings, of people and animals.

Picacho Peak State Park, near Red Rock, encompasses Picacho Peak and Picacho Pass, site of the Civil War's westernmost conflict.

Pipe Spring National Monument, west of Fredonia, is the site of a Mormon ranching settlement and includes a fortlike house called Winsor Castle.

Tombstone Courthouse State Historic Park, in Tombstone, is the restored 1882, red-brick courthouse that was the seat of justice in Arizona's Wild West days.

Golfers at the Paradise Valley Country Club in Phoenix enjoy a view of the Camelback Mountains.

Tubac Presidio State Historic Park, in Tubac, is the site of the Spanish presidio that was the earliest European settlement in Arizona.

Tumacacori National Monument, south of Tubac, contains ruins of the Spanish mission established by Padre Kino in the late 1600s. The church, cemetery, and other remnants date back only to 1800.

Yuma Territorial Prison State Historic Park, in Yuma, includes the remains of the notorious territorial prison built by convicts in 1875 and known as the "hellhole of Arizona."

Other Interesting Places to Visit:

Apache Trail, Arizona 88 through Tonto National Forest, runs through the Superstition Mountains and past many Indian ruins.

Canyon de Chelly National Monument, near Chinle, 26 mi. (42 km) long, contains prehistoric Anasazi cliff dwellings. A group of Navajo Indians now live on the canyon's floor.

Casa Grande Ruins National Monument, north of Coolidge, is a collection of Hohokam villages, among which is a four-story masonry tower.

Grand Canyon, across Arizona's northwest corner, is a magnificent, multicolored gorge, more than 1 mi. (1.6 km) deep, worn through the rocks by the Colorado River over a period of five hundred million years.

London Bridge, in Lake Havasu City, is a reassembled stone bridge brought from London, England.

Lowell Observatory, in Flagstaff, is the observatory from which Clyde Tombaugh discovered the planet Pluto in 1930, using the facility's historic 24-in. (61-cm) Clark refractor telescope.

Meteor Crater, west of Winslow, is the largest preserved meteor crater on earth. It is 570 ft. (174 m) deep and almost 3 mi. (4.8 km) wide. Nearby are the Astronaut Hall of Fame and the Museum of Astrogeology.

Montezuma Castle National Monument, north of Camp Verde, contains the ruins of a five-story, twelfth-century adobe cliff dwelling that rises inside a cave.

Navajo National Monument, on the Navajo Indian Reservation in northeastern Arizona, contains the spectacular Anasazi cave pueblos of Betatakin, Keet Seel, and Inscription House.

Old Tucson, west of Tucson, was the backdrop for the 1939 movie *Arizona* and many other films. Now it is an amusement park with an Old West theme.

Organ Pipe Cactus National Monument, south of Ajo, features organ-pipe and other native cactus species. Along Ajo Mountain and Puerto Blanco scenic drives, visitors can see abundant desert wildlife and rare desert plants.

Petrified Forest National Park, east of Holbrook, was a forest in prehistoric times. Many specimens of petrified trees remain among the park's brilliantly colored hills and valleys.

Saguaro National Monument, east and west of Tucson, contains stands of giant saguaros, the largest cactus species in the world. Hiking trails and scenic drives meander through the monument.

San Xavier del Bac Mission, south of Tucson, called the White Dove of the Desert because of its whitewashed exterior, is a Spanish mission built by Franciscan padres in the late 1700s.

Sunset Crater National Monument, north of Flagstaff, is the site of the giant black cinder cone from Arizona's last erupting volcano.

Tombstone, in Cochise County, is the site of the OK Corral, where Deputy Marshall Wyatt Earp and Doc Holliday had their famous shootout with the Clanton gang in 1881. The town's Boot Hill Graveyard was the final resting place for Billy Clanton and other unfortunate gunslingers.

Tonto National Monument, near Theodore Roosevelt Dam, contains the ruins of fourteenth-century Salado cliff dwellings overlooking Theodore Roosevelt Lake. Exhibits in the visitors' center illustrate the Salados' way of life.

Tuzigoot National Monument, east of Clarkdale, overlooks the Verde River valley and contains several large Sinagua pueblos, one with more than one hundred rooms.

Walnut Canyon National Monument, east of Flagstaff, features over three hundred Sinagua cliff dwellings beneath overhanging canyon walls.

Wupatki National Monument, north of Flagstaff, is a collection of twelfth-century Sinagua ruins, including a sandstone pueblo with more than one hundred rooms, a circular ball court, and a large amphitheater.

IMPORTANT DATES

c. A.D. 1064—Sunset Crater volcano begins its eruption

c. 1350—The Hohokam Indians build Casa Grande in Coolidge

1536—Álvar Núñez Cabeza de Vaca and three companions travel through the American Southwest

1539—Franciscan missionary Marcos de Niza, traveling from Mexico City, crosses Arizona while searching for the legendary Seven Cities of Cibola

1540—Spanish explorer Francisco Vásquez de Coronado leads an expedition into Arizona and claims the Southwest for Spain; Coronado sends Pedro de Tovar into Arizona's Hopi land; García López de Cárdenas is the first European to sight the Grand Canyon

1582-1583—Antonio de Espejo travels through Arizona seeking valuable minerals

1629—Franciscan missionaries establish a mission among the Hopis

1680—In the Pueblo Revolt, the Hopis kill missionary priests and burn churches

1687—Jesuit priest Eusebio Francisco Kino begins missionary work among the Indians in Pimeria Alta, an area that includes southern Arizona

1736—Rich silver deposits are discovered at Arizonac, an arroyo west of Nogales

1751—Pima and Papago Indians of Pimeria Alta revolt against white priests and miners in the area

1752—Arizona's first white settlement is established at Tubac

1768—Spain expels Jesuit missionaries from its New World colonies; Franciscan friar Francisco Tomás Garcés begins missionary work in Arizona

1775—Spanish troops establish a fort at Tucson

1821—Mexico wins independence from Spain; Arizona becomes part of Mexico

1824—Anglo-Americans first enter Arizona to trap beavers

1846—The Mexican War begins; Colonel Stephen Watts Kearny leads the Army of the West through Arizona

1848—The Treaty of Guadalupe Hidalgo ends the Mexican War; Mexico cedes a vast territory that includes most of Arizona to the United States

1850—The New Mexico Territory, including most of Arizona, is created by Congress

1853—In the Gadsden Purchase, the United States buys from Mexico land between the Gila River and Arizona's present southern border

1857—The "Jackass Mail" route opens between San Antonio, Texas, and San Diego, California, bringing stagecoaches through Arizona

1858—The Butterfield Overland Mail route opens, passing through Arizona from Tipton, Missouri, to San Francisco, California

1861—Conflicts break out between the United States Army and the Chiricahua Apaches

1862—Confederate troops under Captain Sherod Hunter occupy Tucson, retreating later in the year; the war's westernmost battle takes place at Picacho Pass

1863—Arizona officially becomes a territory; gold is discovered in the Bradshaw Mountains

1864—Prescott replaces Fort Whipple as Arizona's territorial capital

1867—The territorial capital is moved from Prescott to Tucson

1869—John Wesley Powell makes his first exploration of the Grand Canyon

1876—The infamous Yuma Territorial Prison is opened

1877—Silver is discovered at Tombstone; rail lines begin operation in Arizona; the territorial capital is moved from Tucson back to Prescott

Apache women at their wickiup, 1880

1880 — The Southern Pacific Railroad reaches Tucson

1883 — The Atlantic and Pacific Railroad, part of a transcontinental rail route, crosses northern Arizona

1887 — The Southern Pacific Railroad service extends to Phoenix

1888 — Prescott holds the first rodeo to charge admission and give prizes

1889 — Arizona's territorial capital makes its final move, from Prescott to Phoenix

1902 — The Reclamation Act is passed; construction of Theodore Roosevelt Dam on the Salt River begins

1910 — Congress passes the Arizona Enabling Act, opening the way to statehood; Arizona's constitutional convention convenes

1911 — Theodore Roosevelt Dam is completed

1912 — Arizona becomes the forty-eighth state on February 14

1936—Hoover Dam on the Colorado River is completed

1964—Arizona's Republican senator, Barry Goldwater, runs for president and is overwhelmingly defeated by President Lyndon B. Johnson

1974—The Central Arizona Project is started

1981—Sandra Day O'Connor, an Arizona judge, is the first woman appointed to the United States Supreme Court

1985—The Central Arizona Project begins operation

1988—Governor Evan Mecham is impeached and removed from office; Rose Mofford succeeds him, becoming Arizona's first woman governor

1990—Forest fires sweep through the forests of central Arizona

IMPORTANT PEOPLE

E. F. "NED" BEALE

Juan Bautista de Anza (1735-1788?), Spanish explorer, government official; as Spanish commandant at Tubac, he established a land route between Arizona and Monterey, California (1774); established colonies on the Colorado River in present-day Arizona; founded California's San Francisco colony (1776); Spanish governor of New Mexico (1778-88)

Edward Fitzgerald "Ned" Beale (1822-1893), explorer, surveyor; as a naval officer, he made six trips between Washington, D.C., and California carrying military information during the Mexican War (1846-48); led a railroad surveying team from Fort Defiance, New Mexico, through Arizona to the Colorado River using camels (1857); U.S. minister to Austria-Hungary (1876-77)

Álvar Núñez Cabeza de Vaca (1490?-1560?), Spanish explorer; survivor of a shipwrecked expedition to Florida (1528); explored westward, passing through what is now Arizona (1536); his reports of the expedition led to later explorations by Niza (1539) and Coronado (1540-42)

Christopher "Kit" Carson (1809-1868), trapper, Indian scout; left Kentucky to join expeditions to Santa Fe (1826) and California (1829-31); made his living as a trapper (1831-42), part of the time in Arizona; was a scout for Colonel Stephen Kearny in Arizona during the Mexican War (1846-47); was United States government agent to the Ute Indians (1853-61); commanded Civil War troops against the Indians in the New Mexico Territory

KIT CARSON

Francisco Vásquez de Coronado (1510?-1554), Spanish explorer; led an expedition into present-day Arizona in 1540 while searching for the Seven Cities of Cíbola; claimed much of the Southwest, including present-day Arizona, for Spain; sent exploring parties under García López de Cárdenas, who discovered the Grand Canyon, and Hernando de Alarcón, who discovered the mouth of the Colorado River

GEORGE CROOK

George Crook (1829-1890), army officer; battled Indians in the northwest and southwest United States; broke the power of Arizona's Apaches and Yavapais (1871-73); fought in the Sioux War (1876); lost to Crazy Horse at Rosebud Creek (1876); fought Geronimo's Chiricahua Apaches (1882-85)

Lafayette Maynard Dixon (1875-1946), artist; came to Arizona in the 1890s to sketch and paint landscape scenes, Indians, and other local people; in 1909, created paintings for Tucson's Southern Pacific railway station; lived in Tucson from 1939 until his death

Lewis Williams Douglas (1894-1974), born in Bisbee; businessman, politician; had interests in mining and citrus farming in Arizona; was an officer of a number of financial institutions, chemical and mineral corporations, charitable organizations, and arts and cultural institutions; U.S. representative from Arizona (1927-33); U.S. ambassador to Great Britain (1947-50)

LEWIS W. DOUGLAS

Wyatt Berry Stapp Earp (1848-1929), frontier lawman, gambler; assistant marshal in Dodge City, Kansas (1876, 1878-79); was deputy marshal in Tombstone in 1881 at the time of the legendary gunfight at the OK Corral

Antonio de Espejo (1538-1585?), Spanish merchant, miner, explorer; prospected for precious minerals in Mexico's San Bartolomé Valley; traveled from New Mexico to Arizona's Verde Valley in 1583 prospecting for valuable minerals, thus adding to Spain's information about the territory north of Coronado's expedition

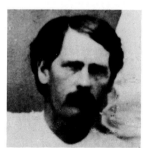

WYATT EARP

BARRY GOLDWATER

ZANE GREY

CARL T. HAYDEN

GEORGE W. P. HUNT

Francisco Tomás Hermenegildo Garcés (1738-1781), Spanish Franciscan missionary, explorer; began missionary work in Mexico's Sonora province in 1768 and ministered to Arizona's Indians through the 1770s; made four expeditions to the Gila and Colorado rivers (1768-74) and founded missions among the Yumas; traveled the Colorado River to its mouth at the Gulf of California (1775); pushed for the opening of a road between northern California and Arizona; killed in an Indian attack on his missions at the Gila and Colorado rivers

Geronimo (1829-1909), born near present-day Clifton; Apache chief; led the Chiricahua Apaches in battles against whites (1877-86); was captured by General George Crook (1882), escaped, and surrendered to General Nelson A. Miles in 1886; dictated his autobiography, *Geronimo's Story of His Life* (1906)

Barry Morris Goldwater (1909-   ), born in Phoenix; politician; U.S. senator (1953-65, 1969-   ); chaired the Senate Armed Services Committee and the Select Committee on Intelligence

John Campbell Greenway (1872-1926), mining engineer; general manager of Calumet and Arizona Copper in Bisbee (1910) and of Cornelia Copper Company in Ajo (1915); developed Arizona's mining and hydroelectric facilities; vice-president of the Cornelia and Gila Bend Railway; helped build the town of Ajo and is buried there

Zane Grey (1872-1939), novelist; toured Arizona (1908) and began writing novels with western themes, including many with Arizona settings; built a cabin on the Mogollon Rim, north of Payson

Sharlot Hall (1870-1943), prose writer, poet; moved from Kansas to Yavapai County at the age of twelve; an impassioned poem she wrote in 1905 aroused Arizonans' determination to seek statehood for Arizona separate from the New Mexico Territory; named territorial historian in 1909, she traveled throughout Arizona collecting historical information; wrote for *Out West* magazine; collections of her poetry were published in *Cactus and Pine* and *Poems of a Ranchwoman*

Carl Trumbull Hayden (1877-1972), born in Tempe; legislator; U.S. representative (1912-27); U.S. senator (1927-69); president pro tem of the Senate (1957-69); his fifty-seven years in Congress set a record for length of service; worked to get the Central Arizona Project through Congress

George Wylie Paul Hunt (1859-1934), politician; became a rancher in the Salt River Valley (1890-1900), during which time he was secretary, then president, of Old Dominion Commercial Company in Globe; member of Arizona's territorial legislature (1892-1910); president of Arizona's constitutional convention (1910); as Arizona's first state governor, served seven terms (1912-19, 1923-29, 1931-33); U.S. minister to Siam (now Thailand) (1920-21)

Helen Hull Jacobs (1908-   ), born in Globe; tennis champion, writer; won numerous national women's tennis singles and doubles championships in the 1930s; was the first to win the U.S. women's singles championship four times in a row; a six-time Wimbledon finalist, she was the Wimbledon singles champion in 1936; her many books include her autobiography, *Beyond the Game* (1936)

HELEN HULL JACOBS

Ulysses Simpson Kay (1917-   ), born in Tucson; composer, educator; composed numerous orchestral, choral, band, and chamber music works; two-time winner of the Rome Prize in Composition (1949-50, 1951-52); member of the first official delegation of composers to the Soviet Union in the U.S. State Department's cultural exchange program (1958)

Eusebio Francisco Kino (1645-1711), Jesuit missionary, explorer; called the Padre on Horseback; from 1687 to 1711 he ministered to the Pima and Papago Indians of Pimeria Alta (northern Mexico and southern Arizona) and founded a number of missions; began Arizona's livestock industry by introducing cattle raising; explored widely in the Southwest; discovered the Casa Grande ruins near Coolidge; wrote an autobiography, *Favores Celestiales* (1708)

PERCIVAL LOWELL

Antoine Leroux (1801?-1861), trapper, scout; blazed trails for many Arizona expeditions, including the Mormon Battalion's roadbuilding expedition during the Mexican War (1846), Lorenzo Sitgreaves's surveying expedition through northern Arizona (1851), and Amiel Whipple's survey along the thirty-fifth parallel (1853)

Percival Lowell (1855-1916), astronomer; came to Arizona in 1893, where he founded Lowell Observatory near Flagstaff; known for his studies of Mars and for predicting the discovery of Pluto, which happened in 1930

EVAN MECHAM

Frank Luke, Jr. (1897-1918), grew up in Phoenix; military aviator; flew fighter planes in World War I; the first pilot to win the Congressional Medal of Honor

Evan Mecham (1924-   ), politician; settled in Arizona after World War II; Arizona state senator (1960-62); a maverick populist, he was elected governor in 1986; in 1988 he was impeached, found guilty of criminal charges, and removed from office

Rose Mofford (1922-   ), born in Globe; state official; assistant to Arizona's secretary of state (1955-75), assistant director of revenue (1975-77), secretary of state (1977-88); upon the impeachment of Governor Evan Mecham in 1988, became acting governor of Arizona and the state's first woman governor

ROSE MOFFORD

SANDRA DAY O'CONNOR

"BUCKY" O'NEILL

WILLIAM H. PICKERING

CHARLES D. POSTON

Frank Morrill Murphy (1854-1917), financier; moved to Arizona in the 1870s to work on the stagecoach line to California; worked with "Diamond Jim" Reynolds in operating the Congress Mine; in the 1890s and early 1900s was the president of the Santa Fe, Prescott and Phoenix Railroad and several other Arizona railways; built the so-called Impossible Bradshaw Mountain Railroad

Marcos de Niza (1495?-1558), called Fray Marcos; Franciscan missionary, explorer; the first European known definitely to have seen Arizona; did missionary work in Peru, Guatemala, and Mexico; traveled through present-day Arizona and New Mexico in 1539 while searching for the legendary Seven Cities of Cibola; was a guide on Francisco de Coronado's 1540 expedition

Sandra Day O'Connor (1930-   ), jurist; opened a private law practice in Phoenix in 1959; state senator (1969-75); senate majority leader (1973-74); sat on Maricopa County's superior court (1975-79) and the Arizona court of appeals (1979-81); associate justice of the United States Supreme Court (1981-   ), the first woman to hold that position

Juan de Oñate (1550?-1630), Spanish explorer; appointed the first Spanish governor of New Mexico (1595), which included present-day Arizona; on military expeditions, traveled to Hopi country (1598); traveled through Arizona once again (1604), searching for a passage to the Pacific Ocean

William O. "Bucky" O'Neill (1860-1898), editor, judge, soldier, sheriff; moved to Arizona from Washington, D.C., in 1880; known for his pursuit of outlaws; a captain in Theodore Roosevelt's Rough Riders in the Spanish-American War, he was the first Arizonan to volunteer for the war and lost his life in the charge up San Juan Hill

Alexander McCarrell Patch (1889-1945), born at Fort Huachuca; army officer; in World War II, commanded the U.S. Seventh Army as it landed in southern France and moved into Germany

James Ohio Pattie (1804-1850?), frontiersman; made several exploring and trapping expeditions in the Southwest, including some in Arizona; his account of his experiences, *Personal Narrative* (1830), is believed to be largely false

William Henry Pickering (1858-1938), astronomer; studied solar eclipses; discovered Phoebe, a satellite of Saturn (1899); working with Percival Lowell, he installed Lowell Observatory's first telescope and dome (1894); predicted, along with Lowell, the existence of a ninth planet (1919)

Charles Debrille Poston (1825-1902), prospector, miner, politician; began exploring southern Arizona for mineral deposits (1854); superintendent of Indian Affairs for Arizona Territory (1863); the Arizona Territory's first delegate to the U.S. Congress (1864-65); known as the Father of Arizona; buried in Phoenix

John Wesley Powell (1834-1902), geologist; led explorations of the Green and Colorado rivers (1869-75), including the Grand Canyon; staff member (1875-81) and director (1881-94) of the U.S. Geological Survey; director of Smithsonian Institution's Bureau of Ethnology (1879-1902); his books include *Exploration of the Colorado River of the West and Its Tributaries* (1875), *An Introduction to the Study of Indian Languages* (1877), and *Report on the Lands of the Arid Region of the United States* (1878)

WILLIAM REHNQUIST

William Hubbs Rehnquist (1924-   ), lawyer, judge; practiced law in Phoenix (1953-69); assistant U.S. attorney general (1969-71); associate justice (1971-86) and chief justice (1986-   ) of the U.S. Supreme Court

Ross Santee (1889-1965), artist, writer; moved to Gila County (1915), where he worked as a ranch hand; drew horses and Arizona landscape scenes; wrote realistic tales of Apaches and cowboys, including *Men and Horses, Cowboy, Lost Pony Tracks*, and *Apache Land*; died in Globe

CLYDE W. TOMBAUGH

Ed Schieffelin (1847-1897), prospector, miner; from 1862 to 1877, prospected for gold throughout the West, arriving at Fort Huachuca in 1877; worked as an Indian scout in 1877; discovered silver in Arizona's San Pedro valley (1877) at what became Tombstone, Arizona's greatest boomtown

John W. (Jack) Swilling (1831-1878), prospector, farmer; while passing through the Salt River Valley in 1867, he discovered prehistoric Hohokam irrigation canals; with investors, he developed the canals to irrigate the surrounding ranches and farms; the resulting community was named Phoenix

Clyde William Tombaugh (1906-   ), astronomer; at Lowell Observatory, discovered the planet Pluto in 1930

MORRIS UDALL

Morris King Udall (1922-   ), born in St. Johns; politician; began practicing law in Tucson in 1949; U.S. representative (1961-   ); keynote speaker at the 1980 Democratic national convention

Stewart Lee Udall (1920-   ), born in St. Johns; politician; began practicing law in Tucson in 1948; U.S. representative (1955-61); as U.S. secretary of the interior (1961-69), was the first Arizonan to serve in a cabinet position; published numerous articles and books on environmental issues, including *National Parks of America, The Quiet Crisis*, and *Agenda for Tomorrow*

STEWART UDALL

Joseph Rutherford (Joe) Walker (1798-1876), trapper, guide; was a guide in John C. Frémont's 1845-46 California expedition; took part in Benjamin Bonneville's 1853 expedition to the Rocky Mountains; led a group into Arizona (1861) and discovered gold in present-day Prescott (1862); Arizona's town of Walker, Nevada's Walker Lake, and California's Walker Pass are named after him

PAULINE WEAVER

FRANK LLOYD WRIGHT

Pauline Weaver (1800-1867), trapper, scout; son of a pioneer father and a Cherokee mother; traveled to Arizona in the early 1830s while working for the Hudson's Bay Company; was a scout and guide on a number of expeditions into Arizona; in 1862, with a party of trappers, he discovered gold in Yuma County; is buried in Prescott

William Sherley ''Old Bill'' Williams (1787-1849), mountain man, trapper; wandered through the West as a Methodist minister; helped survey the Santa Fe Trail (1825-26); in 1826, began trapping in the Gila River area of present-day Arizona; lived with Hopis in 1827 and attempted to convert them to Christianity; joined Joe Walker's 1833-34 expedition to California; guided several expeditions to New Mexico and California (1841-48), including one of John C. Frémont's; the town of Williams and Bill Williams Mountain are named after him

Frank Lloyd Wright (1867-1959), architect; built Taliesin West in Scottsdale as his western home, studio, and architecture school, where he continued developing his architectural ideas; died in Phoenix

Ewing Young (1792?-1841), trapper, colonizer; led a party in battling Pima and Maricopa Indians near the Gila River (1826); led trapping and exploring expeditions to California (1829-32) and one to Yuma (1832)

GOVERNORS

George W. P. Hunt	1912-1917	Ernest W. McFarland	1955-1959
Thomas E. Campbell	1917	Paul Fannin	1959-1965
George W. P. Hunt	1917-1919	Samuel P. Goddard, Jr.	1965-1967
Thomas E. Campbell	1919-1923	John R. Williams	1967-1975
George W. P. Hunt	1923-1929	Raul H. Castro	1975-1977
John C. Phillips	1929-1931	Wesley H. Bolin	1977-1978
George W. P. Hunt	1931-1933	Bruce E. Babbitt	1978-1987
Benjamin B. Moeur	1933-1937	Evan Mecham	1987-1988
Rawleigh C. Stanford	1937-1939	Rose Mofford	1988-1991
Robert T. Jones	1939-1941	Fife Symington	1991-
Sidney P. Osborn	1941-1948		
Dan E. Garvey	1948-1951		
J. Howard Pyle	1951-1955		

Topography

RL 86-S-6

MAP KEY

UTAH · COLO

LINCOLN

Las Vegas
Henderson
Boulder City

St. George
Hurricane
Colorado City
Fredonia
Kanab
Page

GRAND CANYON NATIONAL PARK

NAVAJO INDIAN RESERVATION

HOPI INDIAN RESERVATION

APACHE RESERVATION

Gallup

Kingman
Flagstaff
Winslow
Holbrook
Williams
Sedona

Prescott
Payson
St. Johns

Lake Havasu City
Parker
Wickenburg

Phoenix
Scottsdale
Mesa
Tempe
Chandler
Gilbert
Glendale
Peoria

Globe
Miami
Safford
Clifton
Morenci

Blythe

Yuma
San Luis
Río Colorado
Somerton

Casa Grande
Eloy
Florence
Coolidge

Tucson
S. Tucson

Ajo

Nogales
Nogales
Agua Prieta
Douglas
Bisbee
Sierra Vista
Tombstone
Willcox

MEXICO
SONORA

Caborca
Santa Ana
Magdalena
Cananea
Nacozari
Arizpe
Cumpas
Oputo

CONTINENTAL DIVIDE

Phoenix inset

Morristown
Wittmann
Cave Creek
Surprise
El Mirage
Peoria
Sun City
Glendale
Litchfield Park
Goodyear
Avondale
Buckeye
Valencia
Palo Verde
Phoenix
Tolleson
Scottsdale
Paradise Valley
Tempe
Mesa
Chandler
Gilbert
Higley
Guadalupe
W. Chandler
Ocotillo
Komatke
Apache Jct.
Queen Cr.

A-520503-71
COSMO SERIES ARIZONA
Copyright by
RAND MCNALLY & COMPANY
Made in U.S.A.

Longitude West of Greenwich

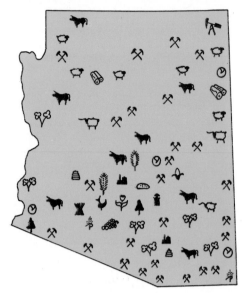

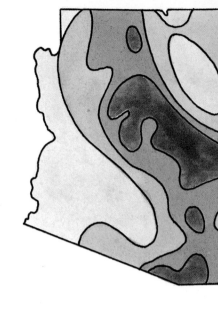

Legend

 FOREST PRODUCTS	POULTRY	POTATOES
NURSERY PRODUCTS	WHEAT	CORN
MANUFACTURING	BARLEY	FRUIT
DAIRY PRODUCTS	SORGHUMS	GRAPES
BEEF CATTLE	COTTON	HONEY
SHEEP	HAY	MINING
ANGORA GOATS	VEGETABLES	OIL

AVERAGE YEARLY PRECIPITATION

Centimeters		Inches
More than 41		More than 16
30 to 41		12 to 16
20 to 30		8 to 12
Less than 20		Less than 8

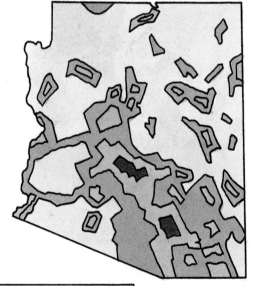

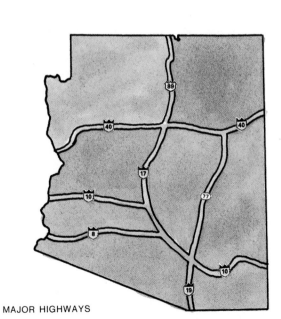

POPULATION DENSITY

Number of persons per square kilometer		Number of persons per square mile
More than 20		More than 50
4 to 20		10 to 50
2 to 4		5 to 10
Less than 2		Less than 5

MAJOR HIGHWAYS

TOPOGRAPHY

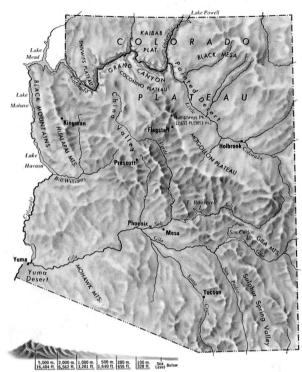

Courtesy of Hammond, Incorporated
Maplewood, New Jersey

COUNTIES

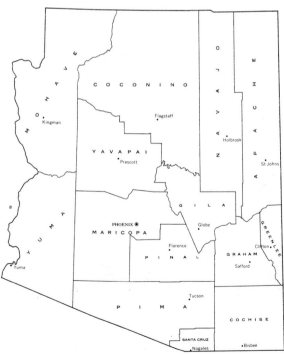

The Pine-Strawberry Archaeological and Historical Society has restored Arizona's oldest standing schoolhouse.

INDEX

Page numbers that appear in boldface type indicate illustrations

Toroweap Point, on the North Rim of Grand Canyon National Park

142

Picture Identifications

Front cover: Palisades of the Desert from Desert View, Grand Canyon National Park
Pages 2-3: A view of the red rocks at Sedona
Page 6: Prickly pear cactus blossoms
Pages 8-9: Table Mountain, Pusch Ridge, Santa Catalina Mountains
Pages 20-21: A montage of Arizonans
Pages 26-27: Keet Seel Ruin, Navajo National Monument
Page 40: A covered wagon and a plow at Pipe Springs National Monument that were typical of the equipment used by the Mormon pioneers who lived at this remote fort
Page 50: Westward Look, a Tucson resort
Page 58: The State Capitol, Phoenix
Pages 68-69: Hopi baskets
Pages 80-81: Coffee Pot Rock, Sedona
Page 108: Montage showing the state flag, the state tree (Paloverde), the state mammal (ring-tailed cat), the state fossil (petrified wood), and the state gemstone (turquoise)
Back cover: Cathedral Rocks and Oak Creek Rock Crossing

About the Author

Ann Heinrichs is a free-lance writer and editor living in Chicago. She has worked for such educational publishers as Encyclopaedia Britannica, World Book Encyclopedia, and Science Research Associates. As a music critic and feature writer, her articles have appeared in various publications. Ms. Heinrichs has written seven books in the *America the Beautiful* series. After several treks through Arizona's deserts, canyons, valleys, and prehistoric ruins, she is hopelessly in love with the state.

Picture Acknowledgments

Front cover: © **Larry Ulrich Photography**; 2-3: © **Bob and Suzanne Clemenz Photography**; 4: © **Larry Ulrich Photography**; 5: © Manley Photo—Tucson/**SuperStock**; 6: © **Bob and Suzanne Clemenz Photography**; 8-9: © **Larry Ulrich Photography**; 11: © Manley Photo—Tucson/**SuperStock**; 12 (both pictures): © **Larry Ulrich Photography**; 13 (both pictures): © **Larry Ulrich Photography**; 14: © Manley Photo—Tucson/**SuperStock**; 15: © **Larry Ulrich Photography**; 17: © **Larry Ulrich Photography**; 18 (both pictures): © **Larry Ulrich Photography**; 19 (top left and right): © **Larry Ulrich Photography**; 19 (bottom left): © **Bob and Suzanne Clemenz Photography**; 19 (bottom right): © **Jerry Jacka Photography, Phoenix**; 20 (top right): © Matt Bradley/**Tom Stack & Associates**; 20 (bottom left): © **Betty Groskin**; 20 (bottom right): © Karl Kummels/**SuperStock**; 21 (top left): © **Christine Keith**; 21 (top right): © **Cameramann International, Ltd.**; 21 (bottom left): © **James Tallon Outdoor Exposures**; 21 (bottom right): © **Jerry Jacka Photography, Phoenix**; 24: © **Bob and Suzanne Clemenz Photography**; 26-27: © **Larry Ulrich Photography**; 29 (both pictures): © **Larry Ulrich Photography**; 30: © **Jerry Jacka Photography, Phoenix**; 31 (both pictures): © **Jerry Jacka Photography, Phoenix**; 33 (both pictures): © **Bob and Suzanne Clemenz Photography**; 34 (both pictures): © **Jerry Jacka Photography, Phoenix**; 37 (left): James P. Rowan; 37 (right): © **Bob and Suzanne Clemenz Photography**; 38 (left): The Bettmann Archive; 38 (right): **Arizona Historical Society/Tucson**; 40: © **Bob and Suzanne Clemenz Photography**; 43: **Arizona Historical Society/Tucson**; 44: The Bettmann Archive; 46: **Arizona Historical Society/Tucson**; 47 (both pictures): **Arizona Historical Society/Tucson**; 48: **Arizona Historical Society/Tucson**; 50: © George Hunter/**SuperStock**; 52: **Arizona Historical Society/Tucson**; 53: © Sal Maimone/**SuperStock**; 54: **Arizona Historical Society/Tucson**; 57 (both pictures): **AP/Wide World Photos**; 58: © Sal Maimone/**SuperStock**; 61: © Manley Photo—Tucson/**SuperStock**; 62: © **SuperStock**; 64: © R.E. Dietrich/**SuperStock**; 65: © **Jerry Jacka Photography, Phoenix**; 66: © Ray Manley/**SuperStock**; 68-69: © **Jerry Jacka Photography, Phoenix**; 71: © **Jerry Jacka Photography, Phoenix**; 73 (top left): © **Jerry Jacka Photography, Phoenix, Courtesy Margaret Kilgore Gallery, Scottsdale, Arizona**; 73 (top right, bottom left, and bottom right): © **Jerry Jacka Photography, Phoenix**; 74: © **Jerry Jacka Photography, Phoenix**; 77: © **James Tallon Outdoor Exposures**; 79: © **Bob and Suzanne Clemenz Photography**; 80-81: © **Bob and Suzanne Clemenz Photography**; 83 (left): © **Mack & Betty Kelley**; 83 (map): **Len Meents**; 84: © **Larry Ulrich Photography**; 85 (inset): © **Joan Dunlop**; 85 (right): © Tom Algire/**SuperStock**; 86 (both pictures): © **Larry Ulrich Photography**; 87 (left): © Manley Photo—Tucson/**SuperStock**; 87 (map): **Len Meents**; 89: © **Jerry Jacka Photography, Phoenix**; 90 (left): © **Bob and Suzanne Clemenz Photography**; 90 (right): © Manley Photo—Tucson/**SuperStock**; 92 (map): **Len Meents**; 92 (right): © **Christine Keith**; 93: © **Bob and Suzanne Clemenz Photography**; 95 (left): © **Bob and Suzanne Clemenz Photography**; 95 (map): **Len Meents**; 96: © **Jerry Jacka Photography, Phoenix**; 97: © **Jerry Jacka Photography, Phoenix**; 98: © **Larry Ulrich Photography**; 99 (left): © George Hunter/**SuperStock**; 99 (map): **Len Meents**; 100 (both pictures): © **Jerry Jacka Photography, Phoenix**; 103 (left): © McKinney/**SuperStock**; 103 (right): © **Bob and Suzanne Clemenz Photography**; 104 (map): **Len Meents**; 104 (right): © **Bob and Suzanne Clemenz Photography**; 107: © Carlos Elmer/**SuperStock**; 108 (background): © **Reinhard Brucker**; 108 (turquoise): © **Jerry Jacka Photography, Phoenix**; 108 (petrified wood): © Mary and Loren Root, FPSA/**Root Resources**; 108 (ring-tailed cat): © Ruth Cordner/**Root Resources**; 108 (flag): **Courtesy Flag Research Center, Winchester, Massachusetts 01890**; 112: © **Jerry Jacka Photography, Phoenix**; 116 (left): © George Hunter/**TSW-Click/Chicago Ltd.**; 116 (right): © Alex Jacobs/**SuperStock**; 119: © **Bob and Suzanne Clemenz Photography**; 121: © **Jerry Jacka Photography, Phoenix**; 125: **Arizona Historical Society/Tucson**; 126: **Arizona Historical Society/Tucson**; 127 (Carson, Crook, and Earp): **Arizona Historical Society/Tucson**; 127 (Douglas): **AP/Wide World Photos**; 128 (Goldwater): **The Bettmann Archive**; 128 (Grey): **AP/Wide World Photos**; 128 (Hayden and Hunt): **Arizona Historical Society/Tucson**; 129 (Jacobs and Mofford): **AP/Wide World Photos**; 129 (Lowell): **Historical Pictures Service, Chicago**; 129 (Mecham): **UPI/Bettmann**; 130 (O'Connor and Pickering): **AP/Wide World Photos**; 130 (O'Neill and Poston): **Arizona Historical Society/Tucson**; 131 (all four pictures): **AP/Wide World Photos**; 132 (Weaver): **Arizona Historical Society/Tucson**; 132 (Wright): **AP/Wide World Photos**; 136: **Len Meents**; 138: © **Bob and Suzanne Clemenz Photography**; 141: © **Bob and Suzanne Clemenz Photography**; back cover: © Tom Algire Photography/**Tom Stack & Associates**